Campaign for Wilson's Creek

The Fight for Missouri Begins

Civil War Campaigns and Commanders Series

Published

Campaign for Wilson's Creek

The Fight for Missouri Begins

Jeffrey L. Patrick

MCWHINEY FOUNDATION PRESS
BUFFALO GAP, TEXAS

Library of Congress Cataloging-in-Publication Data

Patrick, Jeffrey L., 1963–
  Campaign for Wilson's Creek : the fight for Missouri begins /
Jeffrey L. Patrick.
    p. cm.
  Includes bibliographical references and index.
  ISBN-13: 978-1-893114-55-5 (pbk. : alk. paper)
  ISBN-10: 1-893114-55-4 (pbk. : alk. paper)
  1. Wilson's Creek, Battle of, Mo., 1861. 2. Missouri—History—Civil
War, 1861–1865: I. Title.
  E472.23.P37 2011
  973.7'31—dc22

                                                    2008005198

McWhiney Foundation Press
P. O. Box 818
Buffalo Gap, Texas 79508
325.572.3974 • 325.572.3991 (fax)
www.tfhcc.com

Printed in the United States of America

Distributed by Texas A&M University Press Consortium
800.826.8911
www.tamupress.com

ISBN-13: 978-1-893114-55-5
ISBN-10: 893114-55-4

Book Designed by Rosenbohm Graphic Design

CONTENTS

Map Key

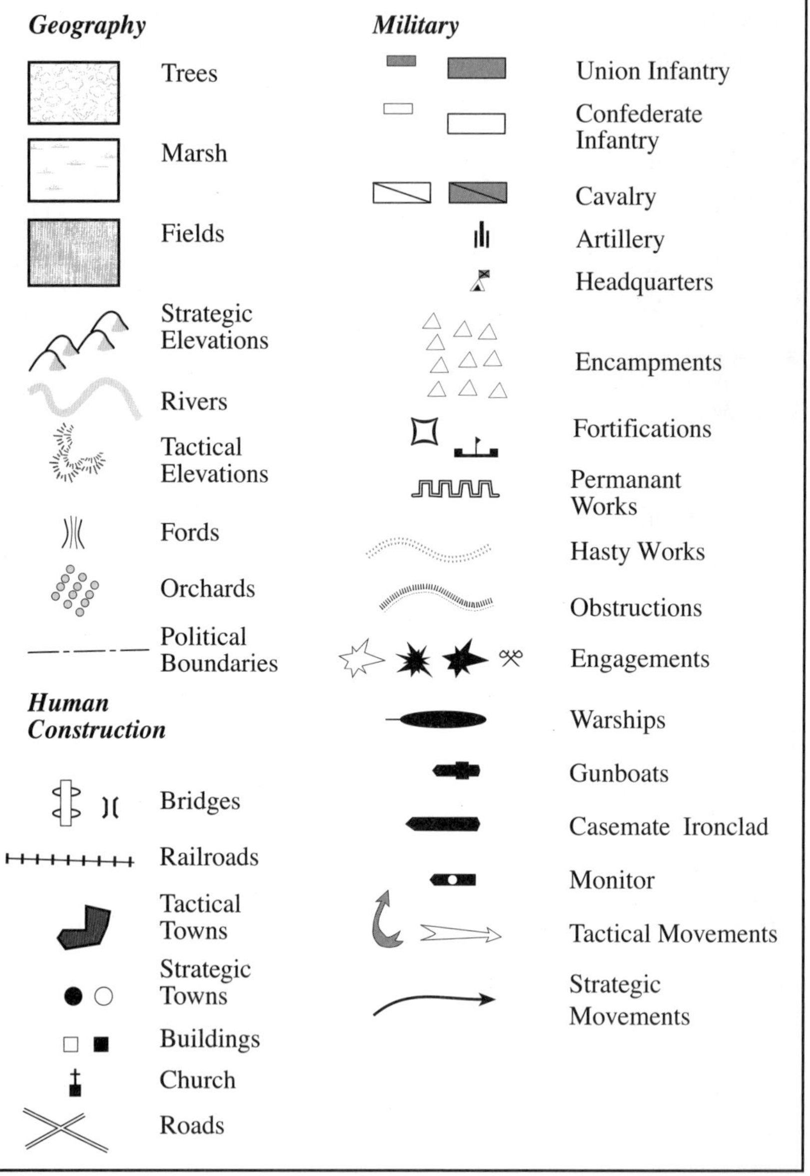

Geography

Trees

Marsh

Fields

Strategic Elevations

Rivers

Tactical Elevations

Fords

Orchards

Political Boundaries

Human Construction

Bridges

Railroads

Tactical Towns

Strategic Towns

Buildings

Church

Roads

Military

Union Infantry

Confederate Infantry

Cavalry

Artillery

Headquarters

Encampments

Fortifications

Permanant Works

Hasty Works

Obstructions

Engagements

Warships

Gunboats

Casemate Ironclad

Monitor

Tactical Movements

Strategic Movements

BIOGRAPHICAL SKETCHES

MAPS

PHOTOGRAPHS

MAJOR PLAYERS

Francis "Frank" P. Blair	Representative, later Colonel of First Missouri Volunteers
Horace Conant	Major, Aide to Nathaniel Lyon
John C. Fremont	Major General
William S. Harney	Brigadier General, Commander of Department of the West
Claiborne Fox Jackson	Governor of Missouri
Abraham Lincoln	US President
Nathaniel Lyon	Captain, later Brigadier General
Benjamin McCulloch	Confederate Brigadier General
James McIntosh	Colonel
Nicholas B. Pearce	Arkansas Brigadier General
Joseph Plummer	Captain US Regulars
Sterling Price	Major General
Franz Sigel	Colonel, Third Missouri Infantry
Thomas L. Snead	Jackson's and then later Price's aide
Samuel Sturgis	Major
Thomas Sweeny	Captain
James Totten	Captain, Battery F, Second US Artillery
William M. Wherry	Aide to Nathaniel Lyon
William E. Woodruff	Captain, Pulaski Battery, Little Rock Arkansas Battery

Campaign for Wilson's Creek

Introduction

On the morning of June 11, 1861, Brig. Gen. Nathaniel Lyon strode through the Planters' House Hotel in Saint Louis, accompanied by Maj. Horace Conant, his aide, and US representative Francis "Frank" P. Blair. The trio were on their way to meet Missouri governor Claiborne Fox Jackson; Maj. Gen. Sterling Price, the commander of the Missouri State Guard; and Thomas L. Snead, one of Jackson's aides. The Planters' House Conference, as it came to be called, was a last desperate effort to prevent Missouri from sliding into full-scale civil war.

Even though the Missouri legislature had authorized Governor Jackson to raise and organize a state militia, the governor agreed in the meeting to disband the pro-Southern Missouri State Guard units that had been formed since early the previous month; to guarantee the protection of pro-Union Missourians; and to prevent Confederate troops from entering the state. Lyon and Blair were asked in return to muster out the pro-Union Home Guard companies they had organized and to guarantee that Federal troops did not occupy any properties beyond those they now held. Price supported the agreement.

Although initially quiet, the passionate Lyon soon entered the fray. He doubted Governor Jackson's desire for peace and questioned whether Missouri's Unionists could be protected with or without the State Guard. The idea that Jackson could prevent Confederate forces from entering Missouri proved to Lyon that the governor was openly negotiating with those in rebellion against the Union. The general could tolerate no one dictating terms to the national government, telling him what a soldier of the US Army could or could not do. Brigadier General Lyon was negotiating from a position of power, and he saw an opportunity to use that power to defeat the governor and his supporters.

After four or five hours of discussion, Lyon had had enough. Although still seated, he spoke slowly, deliberately and, as Snead remembered, "with a peculiar emphasis" to the three Missourians. "'Rather than concede to the State of Missouri for one single instant the right to dictate to my Government in any matter however unimportant, I would' (rising as he said this, and pointing in turn to every one in the room) 'see you, and you, and you, and you, and you, and every man, woman, and child in the State, dead and buried.'" He then turned to Governor Jackson and ended the meeting with these chilling words: "This means war. In an hour one of my officers will call for you and conduct you out of my lines."[1] Lyon then marched out of the room, followed by Major Conant, leaving Representative Blair to bid farewell to the others.

With that dramatic exit, Lyon began a military campaign that would lead to the second major battle of the Civil War and, ultimately, cost him his life. The end of the Planters' House meeting also guaranteed that the long and bitter Civil War in Missouri would now begin in earnest.

What forces had driven the governor of Missouri and a US general to this dramatic confrontation? How was it that the people of Missouri, many of whom were committed to neutrality in the opening weeks of the conflict between North and

South, eventually found themselves fighting a civil war within the larger, national Civil War? How could it be that nearly a century and a half after the meeting at the Planters' House, the names Nathaniel Lyon and Claiborne Fox Jackson continue to spark fierce debate among historians and students of the conflict?

1
Enter the Protagonists

In the summer of 1860, fifty-four-year-old Missouri Democrat Claiborne Fox Jackson was elected governor by a respectable margin, defeating three other candidates. A native Kentuckian, Jackson went to Missouri in the 1820s and soon began an extended career in politics. He was elected to several terms in the Missouri House and Senate, including two stints as House Speaker, and also served as a member of the constitutional convention, state bank commissioner, and state party chairman. Inaugurated as governor on January 3, 1861, during a period of "gloomy apprehension," as he described it, Jackson made his opinions clear in his inaugural address. With one state (South Carolina) having left the Union weeks before President Abraham Lincoln's inauguration, and other states poised to follow, Governor Jackson recognized that the country was in the midst of a serious crisis that had to be resolved.

Although he did not outwardly rationalize secession or suggest that Missouri leave the Union as well, Jackson did argue that any seceding states were not the aggressors and that Missouri would "stand by the South," for the "destiny of the slaveholding States of this Union is one and the same." He also warned that any attempt to force the Southern states to remain in the Union would lead to the "overthrow of our entire Federal system." "The project of maintaining the Federal Government by force may lead to consolidation or despotism, but not to Union," he argued.[1] To gauge the will of the people and Missouri's position in the crisis, the new governor urged that a state convention be called immediately.

The legislature quickly took up Jackson's call. Three groups (avowed secessionists, conditional Unionists, and unconditional Union men) began campaigning for the February 1861 election of delegates. Governor Jackson, Lt. Gov. Thomas Reynolds, and many legislators made up the first group. The second faction, the conditional Unionists, argued that they would support the Union, hoping that there would be congressional guarantees to protect slavery where it existed. However, if such guarantees did not come within a reasonable time, or if the national government made war on any Southern state, they cautioned, then Missourians should side with fellow slave states to resist aggression and take up arms. The final group, primarily German-Americans and their allies in Saint Louis, led by Republican representative Francis "Frank" P. Blair, believed that no matter what occurred, the Union was paramount and should be maintained and defended.

Jackson clearly saw that the secession crisis presented him with a unique opportunity. Having stated his position to his fellow Missourians, he carefully laid plans for the state's secession. He facilitated the appearance before the legislature of a representative from Mississippi who had come to invite Missouri to join the other seceding states. He instructed his lieutenant governor to hold a mass pro-Southern rally in Saint Louis, which led to the organization of secessionist paramilitary companies known as "Minute Men." The governor also

CLAIBORNE FOX JACKSON

Born in Kentucky in 1806, Jackson moved to central Missouri in the 1820s and became a merchant before he developed an interest in politics. He was elected as a Democrat to the Missouri House of Representatives in 1836 and 1842, chosen Speaker of the House in 1844, and was reelected in 1846. In 1848 he was elected to the Missouri Senate and to the Missouri House in 1852; in 1860 he was elected governor of Missouri. In June 1861, Jackson was deposed by Brig. Gen. Nathaniel Lyon; but in July 1861 Governor Jackson commanded Missouri State Guard forces at the Battle of Carthage, Missouri. Following Carthage, he traveled to Little Rock, Memphis, and Richmond to rally Confederate support for the Missouri cause. Jackson was present for the State Guard victory at Lexington, Missouri, in September 1861 and presided over the "rump" (deposed) state legislature that met in Neosho, Missouri, and passed an ordinance of secession in October 1861. After Missouri was accepted into the Confederacy by the Confederate Congress, Jackson traveled to New Orleans; he was present for the Confederate defeat at Pea Ridge, Arkansas, in March 1862. Suffering from stomach cancer, Jackson died on December 7, 1862, from pneumonia.

sent one of his militia officers to meet with the commander of the Federal arsenal in Saint Louis to urge him to surrender peacefully when Missouri seceded.

But Jackson's plans went awry the following month when the votes for convention delegates were counted. Conditional and unconditional Unionist candidates won nearly 110,000 votes, the secessionists less than a third that number. No staunch secessionist candidate was elected to the ninety-nine-man convention. "The result was a surprise to every one," Jackson's aide Thomas L. Snead said, "and a bitter disappointment to the South."[2]

On February 28, the convention met in Jefferson City and elected Sterling Price, a former Missouri governor, congressman, and Mexican War general, as president. Because of inadequate space and the fear of pro-secession influence, the delegates voted to move. On March 4, the day of Lincoln's inauguration, they reconvened in Saint Louis. Within a few days, the delegates voted overwhelmingly that "no adequate cause" existed to compel Missouri to leave the Union. On March 22, the convention adjourned, having earned a place in US history as the only state political convention to meet that spring and actually vote *against* secession. Although it appeared that the people's representatives had spoken with one voice and that Governor Jackson had been thwarted in his efforts to have his state join the Confederacy, that astute politician knew that it was only a temporary setback. By biding his time and avoiding rash acts, Jackson needed only to wait for another opportunity to surface; with the rapidly changing national situation, his chances for success were sure to increase.

Into this unstable situation came Capt. Nathaniel Lyon, the other major player in the tragic drama that was Missouri in the spring of 1861. The forty-two-year-old West Point graduate—a career army officer and the commander of Company B, Second US Infantry—arrived in Saint Louis with his men on February 6. Stationed since the previous December in Fort Scott, Kansas Territory, Lyon and his regulars had been charged with preventing armed conflict between pro-slavery and Free State elements in that region. Now they were ordered to bolster the defenses of the Saint Louis Arsenal, the large government facility where valuable small arms, artillery, ammunition, and other military matériel were assembled and stored for the Indian-fighting army.

If Missouri was a potential powder keg in early 1861, Saint Louis could be considered its fuse. By 1860, Saint Louis County contained 190,000 people, including whites and African Americans, both slave and free. Of that number, 186,000 were free. Just over half (96,000) of its free population was foreign born, principally Germans and Irish, with more than half of that number from the various German states. Indeed, the foreign-born residents of the state were concentrated in Saint Louis County. The immigrant population of no other Missouri county even remotely approached the large number in Saint Louis. Although former citizens of various European nations were living in Missouri, those born in the German states made up the largest number of foreign born in the 1860 census (some 88,000).[3]

In contrast to the native-born, Southern-leaning residents of Saint Louis County, the German element was strongly anti-secession and anti-slavery in sentiment in the spring of 1861. In fact, in the 1860 presidential election, Lincoln and the Republican Party won only two Missouri counties—one was Saint Louis, due in large part to the German-American vote. The reasons behind the German support of Lincoln and the Union were many and complex, but as German newspaper editor Henry Boernstein explained, his countrymen "had no desire to transform the splendid, dignified union of the United States into a mass of independent, petty state sovereignties" similar to those they had left in the old country. In addition, although the Germans of Saint Louis had little direct interaction with slavery, they resented an institution that concentrated power in a "slaveholding elite" and guaranteed that "all political and legal institutions were predicated on the maintenance and promotion" of slavery.[4]

To some native-born Missourians in Saint Louis, on the other hand, the Germans were not only an alien group that spoke an alien language but they were also now a powerful pro-Republican and anti-slavery force, well organized and led. To their opponents in the state, they became the "damned Dutch" (the US corruption of *Deutsche*). That hatred would only quicken as the Germans became increasingly committed to thwarting any secessionist efforts to tear Missouri from the Union.

2
Saint Louis Prepares for War

Despite the vote against secession by the state convention in March 1861, both Gov. Claiborne Fox Jackson's supporters and the German-Americans of Saint Louis continued to forge ahead with their respective plans. The paramilitary "Minute Men" began to parade through the city with fifes and drums, "making dreadful threats against Germans and other citizens loyal to the Union."[1] The Germans countered by forming their own illegal military companies, obtaining arms from pro-Union citizens, and drilling in the secrecy of their "Turner Society" hall (the German-American *Turnverein*, or athletic and social club), houses, and businesses.

National events soon ratcheted up the pressure on both sides. On April 12, 1861, Confederate forces fired on the US garrison of Fort Sumter in Charleston, South Carolina. Three days later, President Abraham Lincoln called for 75,000 three-month volunteers to put down the rebellion, and Jackson was asked to furnish his share of four regiments. Jackson

Members of the St. Louis Turnverein, 1860.

responded in a strongly worded message on April 17: "Your requisition, in my judgment, is illegal, unconstitutional, and revolutionary in its object, inhuman and diabolical, and cannot be complied with. Not one man will the State of Missouri furnish to carry on any such unholy crusade."[2]

Three days later, as if to underscore Governor Jackson's refusal, Missouri secessionists seized the Missouri Depot near Liberty, hauling off sixteen artillery pieces, hundreds of small arms, thousands of rounds of ammunition, and assorted military equipment. Although Jackson's defiant response and the seizure of the depot buoyed secessionist hopes, the Germans of Saint Louis and Capt. Nathaniel Lyon intended to answer Lincoln's call and prevent any further losses of Federal property.

In the two months since his arrival in Saint Louis to defend the arsenal, Lyon had recognized that the enthusiastic Germans were potentially powerful allies. He met and struck up a friendship with Rep. Francis "Frank" P. Blair, who became a colonel late in April and then attended drill sessions of the Turner "Home Guards" to assist with their training and organization.

For some time, Lyon had suspected that the secessionists were planning to strike the Saint Louis Arsenal, a tempting target with a large supply of muskets, artillery, ammunition, and other supplies. After the secessionist raid on the Missouri Depot, Lyon knew he had to act quickly, even if that meant not consulting with his superior, Brig. Gen. William S. Harney, commander of the Department of the West. Not only did the elderly general have no official authorization either to muster the Germans into service or to issue them arms from the arsenal, but he also wished to avoid a possible confrontation at all costs.

Captain Lyon and Colonel Blair would not wait for such permission to come from Harney—they would seek it from higher authorities. On April 21, Blair received permission from the US Secretary of War's office to muster the volunteers and use them to protect the arsenal. That night, the process commenced, as volunteers streamed into the arsenal, were sworn in, and armed. Col. Henry Boernstein, one of the new recruits, wrote that "our march through the city excited some admiration and some distress, in that we were greeted in American neighborhoods with mockery and threats, and in the German areas with cries of jubilation."[3] By late the next day, some seven hundred men had been accepted into US service and placed in defensive positions in the arsenal. Lyon scored a second coup as well: as he enlisted the Germans, orders arrived relieving Harney of command and making Lyon the new department commander.

But Lyon was not content with just defending the arsenal. Knowing that dispersing the arsenal's store of weapons would make it less likely to be attacked, he wrote to Illinois governor Richard Yates on April 16, asking him to requisition "a large supply of arms" for his state's volunteers. Yates did as asked, and Secretary of War Simon Cameron approved the issue of 10,000 arms just four days later. On the night of April 25, Lyon began loading the weapons on board a steamship, the *City of Alton*. Convinced by the ship's captain that all the guns not needed for the arsenal's defense should be moved as well, Lyon ordered another 10,000 muskets, 500 carbines, 500

NATHANIEL LYON

Born in Connecticut in 1818, Lyon graduated from the US Military Academy in 1841, eleventh in his class. He was appointed second lieutenant Second Infantry and was stationed in Florida during the Second Seminole War. In 1847 he was promoted to first lieutenant and participated in Gen. Winfield Scott's Mexico City Campaign, including the battles of Cerro Gordo, Contreras, and Churubusco, and was wounded when his regiment entered Mexico City. That same

year he was appointed brevet captain for his gallantry in Mexico. He was stationed in California in 1849; in 1850 he skirmished with American Indians at Clear Lake. Lyon was again promoted in 1851 to captain, then transferred to the Kansas Territory in 1854. In February 1861 he arrived in Saint Louis with his company to reinforce the Federal arsenal there. In May 1861, Lyon forced the surrender of a Missouri State Militia encampment at Camp Jackson; as a result, he was promoted to brigadier general of volunteers. His force occupied Jefferson City, Missouri's capital, and defeated the Missouri State Guard at the Battle of Boonville in June 1861. While leading the Army of the West, Lyon was killed in action at the Battle of Wilson's Creek; he was the first Union general to die in combat during the Civil War. Lyon is buried in Phoenixville, Connecticut. His actions in Missouri have been debated since his death. Contemporaries such as Thomas L. Snead believed he saved the state for the Union, whereas some modern historians argue that although he could be credited with securing both the Saint Louis Arsenal and Jefferson City, Lyon's aggressive campaign helped polarize the state and led to bitter, fratricidal conflict in Missouri.

revolvers, 2 artillery pieces, and 110,000 cartridges brought on board. Early the next morning, without the knowledge of the pro-Southern Minute Men, 21,000 arms were shipped to Alton, Illinois, and then loaded on a train for transport to Springfield, Illinois. Once again, Lyon had acted decisively to protect the Saint Louis Arsenal and bolster the Union cause in Saint Louis. But to Governor Jackson and his subordinates, this was but a minor setback.

3

BLOOD ON THE STREETS

While Capt. Nathaniel Lyon mustered his volunteers into
Federal service and commandeered the arsenal's weapons, Gov. Claiborne Fox Jackson did not remain idle. On
April 17, he sent two of his militia officers with a message
to Confederate president Jefferson Davis in Montgomery,
Alabama, asking for the loan of heavy artillery to batter down
the walls of the Saint Louis Arsenal. Davis replied six days
later, confirming "the great importance of capturing the arsenal and securing its supplies." He loaned the Missourians two
12-pound howitzers and two 32-pound guns taken from the US
arsenal in Baton Rouge, Louisiana.

At the urging of Missouri State Militia brigadier general
Daniel Marsh Frost, Jackson ordered the militia of Saint
Louis to gather for "training" on May 3. Although Frost
intended to camp his troops and place his artillery on the
commanding ground near the arsenal, Lyon moved his men
to the area first. Undeterred, Frost now fixed his camp on

the western edge of the city at a place called Lindell Grove. There the technically "legal" gathering of militiamen could still counter the buildup of Lyon's forces. The stage was set for a confrontation in Saint Louis.

On the morning of May 6, Frost's First Brigade of Missouri Volunteer Militia (two regiments of infantry, three troops of cavalry, an artillery and an engineer unit) marched into "Camp Jackson" in Lindell Grove. Bearing names such as the "Dixie Guards" and the "Washington Blues," these were not ill-disciplined, nonuniformed citizen soldiers; instead, they were independent militia companies, well dressed and armed. Although many might be described as pro-secessionist in sympathy, a number were, in fact, either sympathetic to the Union cause or, at the very least, neutral in sentiment. The militiamen soon established a formal military camp with dozens of tents, settled into the routine of camp life, and began recruiting interested volunteers, who were no doubt impressed by the martial appearance of Frost's men.

Captain Lyon kept a close watch on the soldiers in Camp Jackson. Early on May 9, he learned that a curious cargo had arrived in Saint Louis and had been delivered to the encampment. His informants explained that crates marked "marble" were now stacked near Brigadier General Frost's headquarters tent. Not only was the presence of marble in a military camp unusual, but its arrival in the dead of night also made it suspicious.[1] Lyon decided to investigate. Realizing that he would be immediately recognized when he approached the encampment, he supposedly adopted an unusual disguise. Col. Francis "Frank" P. Blair's blind mother-in-law, Mira Alexander, was accustomed to taking daily drives in the city. On the afternoon of May 9, prominent Unionist John J. Witzig showed "Mrs. Alexander" around Camp Jackson. In reality, the heavily veiled "woman" was Lyon, clutching a brace of pistols. Lyon's disguise worked—he was able to have a thorough look at Frost's camp without being discovered.

DANIEL M. FROST

Born in New York in 1823, Frost graduated from the US Military Academy in 1844, fourth in his class of twenty-five; commissioned a second lieutenant and posted to the artillery, he later transferred to the Mounted Rifles. He served on the frontier and won a brevet during the Mexican War; after an assignment to Europe, Frost resigned from the army as a first lieutenant and settled in Saint Louis, where he engaged in business, served in the Missouri legislature, and sat on the US Military Academy's Board of Visitors. A brigadier general of state troops at the outbreak of the Civil War, Frost was active in support of Missouri secession. In May 1861 he was compelled to surrender Camp Jackson to the Unionists under Nathaniel Lyon; exchanged, he joined Maj. Gen. Sterling Price's army in southwest Missouri. He commanded Missouri state troops in the Battle of Pea Ridge, Arkansas, in March 1862, after which he raised an artillery brigade that he took across the Mississippi. At Corinth, he served briefly as Gen. Braxton Bragg's inspector general; promoted to brigadier general, C.S.A., in October 1862, to rank from the previous March, Frost was returned to the Trans-Mississippi Theater; he commanded a division in Gen. Thomas C. Hindman's army at Prairie Grove, Arkansas, in December 1862. Frost commanded a division for much of 1863 and took part in the unsuccessful defense of Little Rock. In the fall of 1863, Frost left the army to join his family who had fled to Canada after being banished from their home near Saint Louis. Apparently, Frost failed to submit a formal resignation or to receive authorization for a leave and was dropped from the army rolls in December 1863. After the war, he returned to Saint Louis County, where he engaged in farming until his death in 1900.

Lyon returned from Camp Jackson convinced that the militiamen were a risk to the city and the arsenal; the time had come to bring overwhelming force to bear on Frost's troops. He also knew that Brig. Gen. William S. Harney had been reinstated and would return very soon to take command of the department. Lyon met with the leaders of the Union cause in Saint Louis on the night of May 9 to plead his case. Capturing the militia, he argued, would force Governor Jackson to recognize national authority. Besides, he told them, the camp was "made up for the most part of what has for a long time been known as a body of rabid and violent opposers of the General Government, and who have, during this time, been a terror to all loyal and peaceful citizens." Their "extraordinary and unscrupulous conduct, and their evident design, and of the governor of this State, to take a position of hostility to the United States" was well documented, Lyon explained. Now that the militia had the "means for seizing Government property and overturning its authority," military action was necessary. With only one objection, all those present agreed.[2]

By May 10, Lyon had at his disposal five regiments of US volunteers, five regiments of US Reserve Corps troops (Home Guards), four companies of US regulars, and a volunteer artillery battery. Although some of the volunteer officers had made impressive headway training their new recruits in just two weeks, the volunteers were still quite green. Col. Henry Boernstein explained that although the majority of the new officers and enlisted men had been soldiers in Europe, they had served in the armies of a number of different nations. The rest were completely unfamiliar with firearms. "It was no simple thing," Boernstein wrote, "to unite all these elements into a well-disciplined, harmonious whole and initiate them in American procedure in a matter of days." Lyon decided to leave two companies of regulars and a regiment of volunteers at the arsenal, post two battalions of the Home Guards at the approaches to the arsenal, and gather another full regiment of unarmed Home Guards at their headquarters. Simple thing or not, Lyon assembled a strike force of some seven thousand men to face an estimated nine hundred militiamen.[3]

On the morning of May 10, Captain Lyon rode in front of the troops, delivered "a brief, forceful address," and ordered them to load their weapons.[4] Many of his men did not have uniforms or even proper cartridge boxes, so they carried their cartridges and percussion caps in their pockets. Early that afternoon, the Federal volunteers and regulars marched out of the arsenal toward Camp Jackson. A member of the Third Missouri Infantry, Sgt. Otto C. Lademann, described his regiment's departure: "At about one o'clock the head of our column marched out of the arsenal, led by our regimental band, playing a gay march, our national colors proudly fluttering in the soft balmy May breeze. If we did present a rather motly [sic] appearance in our simple citizen's garb, our shining new muskets and their glittering bayonets, sparkled brightly in the rays of the sun and with proud steps we eagerly marched forward to strike the first offensive blow in St. Louis."[5]

Thomas Gantt, a prominent Unionist, heard of the march of the Federal troops and rode out to see if he could prevent bloodshed. He met Colonel Blair at the head of his First Missouri Volunteers. Blair told Gantt that he was on a "fool's errand," that what Lyon was doing was the only thing to promote the safety of Missouri, "and that to omit doing it would be to allow the conflagration already kindled to involve us in destruction." When Gantt suggested that there was still time to use legal means to resolve the crisis, Blair snapped, "We have no time now for such trifling—the day for such foolery has passed."[6]

Although initially greeted with waves, tears, and cheers, Lyon's Germans soon encountered "a dead and ominous silence," broken only by curses, as they moved toward their objective.[7] "Frequent insulting remarks" were hurled at the troops, with the German volunteers receiving "the great portion."[8] To prevent the escape of the militia, Lyon had wisely arranged his men into several columns, to converge on all four sides of the camp at the same time.

Informants had alerted Brigadier General Frost that Captain Lyon was marshaling his forces and preparing to march. On the morning of May 10, he sent a message to Lyon. Frost acknowledged that he had heard Lyon was concerned that the militia would attack the arsenal and his troops and

FRANCIS P. BLAIR

Born in Kentucky in 1821, Blair graduated from Princeton in 1841, studied law at Transylvania University in Kentucky, and opened a practice in Saint Louis. He staunchly opposed secession and the expansion of slavery into the territories and actively worked against both; he served two terms in the US House of Representatives and was a strong supporter of Abraham Lincoln; his brother Montgomery was Lincoln's first postmaster general. Blair led Missouri's pro-Union faction and with Nathaniel Lyon directed the seizure of pro-secession forces at Camp Jackson;

largely at his own expense Blair raised seven regiments for Federal service and in August 1862 was appointed brigadier general of US Volunteers. He was promoted to major general in November 1862 and commanded a brigade, and then a division, during the Vicksburg Campaign. Later during the Chattanooga Campaign he headed the Fifteenth Corps, Army of the Tennessee; as commander of the Seventeenth Corps, he performed with marked distinction during the Atlanta Campaign of 1864 and played a major role in the July Battle of Atlanta. Blair continued to direct the Seventeenth Corps during Gen. William T. Sherman's March to the Sea and in the Carolinas Campaign of 1865 but resigned his volunteer commission in November 1865. At war's end Blair was financially ruined, having spent his personal fortune in support of the Union; he also fell into disfavor with radical Republicans for his opposition to heavy-handed reconstruction policies. Blair, who favored more lenient readmission terms for Confederate states, was twice nominated for governmental posts by President Andrew Johnson, but he failed to win confirmation from the vindictive Senate. Finally, in 1871 he was selected to fill an unexpired term in the US Senate, but long plagued by poor health, he resigned in 1873. He died in Saint Louis in 1875. Blair was one of several civilian or "political" generals to render excellent service during the Civil War.

was about to strike. Frost argued that Lyon had no justification to attack men "in the lawful performance of duties . . . under the Constitution" and that the idea of an attack on national property by the state militia "has never been entertained" by anyone at the camp. "I would be glad to know from you personally whether there is any truth in the statements," Frost asked. He hoped that both commanders would be able to "keep far from our borders the misfortunes which so unhappily afflict our common country."[9] Frost's messenger arrived at the arsenal just as the troops began their march, but Lyon refused to read the dispatch.

By 3:15 p.m., the Federal columns had converged on Camp Jackson. Although Lyon had hoped that all the columns would be perfectly synchronized, the heat of the day and the length of the march had led to delays. Capt. Thomas Sweeny said "there was not 10 minutes' difference between the arrival of the first and of the last column," but the Federals on the south side were just late enough in arriving to allow perhaps a third of the militiamen to flee.[10] Lyon's men soon closed in around the camp and sealed off all escape. Lyon then sent Frost a demand for immediate surrender. In his note, Lyon stated that the militiamen were "evidently hostile to the Government of the United States" and that the camp was made up of secessionists plotting to seize government property, men openly communicating with the Confederacy, and those who had received stolen government property from the Confederates. Frost had thirty minutes to comply. His only assurance from Lyon was that the militiamen would be "humanely and kindly treated."

Frost quickly called a conference of his officers and asked for a personal meeting with Lyon. The angry captain refused, sending one final note: if Frost did not surrender in ten minutes, Lyon's men would open fire. Frost angrily replied in his own final message: "I never for a moment conceived the idea that so illegal and unconstitutional a demand . . . would be made by any officer of the United States army." But since he was "wholly unprepared to defend my command from this unwarranted attack," he would surrender.[11] The regulars in Lyon's command had been given strict orders not to cheer, or even speak. "Not so with the enthusiastic volunteers," wrote

Spencer Brown, a regular recruit. "Cheer after cheer went up from the assembled crowds, each intent upon screaming the loudest."[12]

Despite the euphoria of Captain Lyon's men, the actual surrender was remarkably peaceful. Clearly, some Unionists were disappointed that the militiamen had not put up a fight, and some of Brigadier General Frost's officers looked "exceedingly disheartened," but most of the militiamen were willing to cooperate. As Sergeant Lademann recalled, "The behavior of both parties was decorous and gentlemanly," with "slight bantering jokes" exchanged between the men in the ranks.[13] Captain Sweeny shook hands with Frost and some of his officers, and the Missouri general remarked that if not for the presence of the regulars, "there would be bloody work," as the militiamen had no feelings against the professional soldiers but certainly despised the volunteers.[14] Captain Lyon gave the militiaman an opportunity to take the oath of allegiance and be paroled, but only ten agreed to do so. The others had already sworn allegiance to the United States, and to their way of thinking, to do it again would be to admit they had been in rebellion.

Although Frost's nearly seven hundred militiamen had been cowed into surrender, Lyon was quickly forced to worry about a much more dangerous enemy. A large crowd of civilians had taken an obvious interest in the events at Camp Jackson. "The news of the movement [of troops] created a deep and profound sensation throughout the city," reported one newspaper, "causing a general closing of stores, and a flocking of the population in the rear of the columns."[15] Some were merely curious onlookers. Others had friends and relatives in the militia ranks and were upset by the turn of events. By another account, "Numbers of men seized rifles, shotguns, or whatever other weapons they could lay hands upon and rushed pell-mell to the assistance of the State troops." Now the hills in the area were "literally black with people," including hundreds of women and children who believed they were out of harm's way.[16] Lyon decided to march his prisoners through this potentially hostile crowd and back to the arsenal—in hindsight, an unfortunate decision but hardly a surprising one because every action the Federal commander took that day was calculated to impress upon the militiamen and the civilians the power of the national authorities.

Preparations were finally completed for the march, and with colors flying and drums beating, Frost led his men out of the camp and onto Olive Street. Captain Lyon's men were drawn up in a hollow square facing the prisoners. Soon an unexplained halt was called, and a German officer came through the ranks of the prisoners demanding the swords of all the officers. Because the terms of surrender had allowed officers to retain their side arms, militia colonel John Knapp protested the order, not wishing to give up a valuable sword given to him by his command. When his protest fell on deaf ears, Knapp broke the sword over a fence post.

Unfortunately for Lyon and his men, the halt lasted for two or three hours, and the crowd used the time to grow more aggressive. "As all St. Louis was excited to madness that day," Frost later explained, "the wild excitement of the unthinking crowd and the animosity of the raw, undisciplined troops were rapidly increasing."[17]

The situation quickly deteriorated, and in the words of one US regular, "a row seemed almost inevitable."[18] "Injurious and insulting remarks were hurled from the crowd," and the "military appearance [of the Federal troops] was criticized and ridiculed," Frost admitted.[19]

Some of the crowd apparently pressed forward, trying to break the ranks of those guarding the militia prisoners. Leveled bayonets initially kept the civilians back, but soon the crowd moved closer.[20] Some in the crowd began throwing rocks, dirt, and sticks at the soldiers. Others apparently pulled pistols and began firing. Undoubtedly several such incidents occurred at more or less the same time. Whatever the provocation, some Federal troops began firing into the crowd, and the effect rippled through the ranks as other companies, no doubt believing that orders had been given to open fire, loosed deadly volleys.[21] Although the officers quickly stopped the firing, after perhaps only two or three minutes, the damage was done.

"The whole commons were covered with a mass of fleeing men, women, horses and vehicles of all kind, all running pell-mell down the line of our regiment for the shelter of the city," wrote one volunteer.[22] In their wake, twenty-eight men, women, and children lay dead or mortally wounded. Three militiamen and three enlisted men and an officer in the Federal ranks were either killed outright or fatally wounded. Scores more in the crowd were wounded but survived. "The wounded and dying made the late beautiful field look like a battle-ground," wrote one eyewitness, "and a more fearful and ghastly sight is seldom seen."[23]

The question of responsibility for what became known as the "Camp Jackson massacre" has been debated ever since the musket smoke dissipated over Lindell Grove. It is clear that although it was a legal assembly, the camp was not entirely "a harmless display of the city military."[24] Certainly, some members of the encampment were secessionists. Although Brigadier General Frost denied the assertion, some pro-Union men accused the militiamen of naming streets *Beauregard* and *Davis* and flying Confederate flags. It is also clear that Frost was harboring military goods stolen from a US arsenal. But it is also true that the militiamen had committed no overtly hostile acts, and the encampment was scheduled to be disbanded within a few days.

Although it can be argued that Captain Lyon used great skill and precision in capturing Frost's militia, the true cause of the riot lies both in his decision to march the prisoners back through the city and the unexplained delay in moving them from the camp. "The facts, the actual facts in the case, were the subject of much inquiry and discussion," said an editorial in the Saint Louis *Weekly Missouri Democrat*, but the editor quite accurately explained that the eyewitness accounts were as "various and conflicting as the political sympathies of the relators." Some eyewitnesses claimed that the troops simply opened fire on unarmed men, women, and children without provocation. Others testified that only insults were thrown. Still others swore that insults and rocks were hurled but that no one fired at the troops. Finally, some asserted that rocks and insults were thrown and pistols fired. It is possible that all the eyewitnesses spoke the truth as they understood it, although human nature, the *Democrat* stated, reasoned that troops would not fire upon a crowd "without *great provocation*." Given that the Germans or "Dutch" were the subjects of "an intense and unreasoning prejudice" and that many in the crowd were sympathetic to the militiamen, such provocation was clearly evident.[25] Once Lyon made the unfortunate decision to march from the camp, an ugly incident became almost unavoidable as the new, undisciplined troops mixed with angry citizens.

The march of the prisoners soon resumed toward the arsenal, where once again the prisoners refused to be paroled. By the evening of May 11, however, all agreed to parole and were released (except one officer who insisted on being treated as a prisoner of war). In the space of a few minutes, the streets of Saint Louis had been covered with casualties, and in Frost's words, "the reputed sins of Camp Jackson" were "avenged" with blood.[26] In reality, both Governor Jackson and Captain Lyon had won: Jackson now had a powerful rallying cry to take to the Missouri legislature, and Lyon had reasserted US authority in Saint Louis by the bayonet. But a contemporary historian summarized the true legacy of Camp Jackson: the incident produced "a feeling of bitter hostility" that "desolated half the State of Missouri with fire and sword, and deluged it in the blood of its best and bravest citizens."[27]

4
AFTERMATH

Hysteria gripped Saint Louis in the wake of the Camp Jackson "massacre." Many fled the city, while some took to the streets to attend hastily formed rallies. Others closed their businesses and barricaded themselves in their homes to wait out the storm. Rumors ran wild. The city was "trembling upon the verge of anarchy," said one resident. Although the streets were thronged with men, "each stared at all the rest as if he feared a secret stab or open assault." "Conversation was suppressed . . . or carried on in that deep undertone that presages tumult and disaster." One rumor spread that the German troops had revolted and were preparing to sack and burn the city. A similar rumor had swept through the German neighborhoods that the secessionists were planning the same course of action.[1] "In some parts of the city a perfect panic prevailed," one newspaper said. "Had there been notice of a destructive hurricane or an earthquake about to visit the city, there could scarcely have been a more disturbed sense of impending peril than existed in many quarters."[2]

The violence flared again late on the afternoon of May 11, when a Federal Reserve Corps regiment that did not participate in the events at Camp Jackson was accosted by a mob while marching homeward. In a repeat of the day before, civilians fired shots at the soldiers, and the inexperienced troops fired into the civilians. Four members of the Reserve Corps were killed and five civilians left dead or mortally wounded. Several more were injured.

Brig. Gen. William S. Harney, recently restored to command of the Department of the West, arrived back in Saint Louis the day after the Camp Jackson episode, just in time to witness the attack on the Reserve Corps men. He found the city to be "in a greatly excited state."[3] On May 12, he issued a proclamation, which he was assured was "well received" and "had the effect to tranquilize the public mind."[4] In it, he wrote that although he deplored the events of the previous few days, he was determined to deal with the present and future and preserve the public peace. He urged the people to "abstain from the excitements of public meetings and heated discussions." Two days later, Harney issued a more formal message. "Missouri must share the destiny of the Union," he wrote, and the whole power of the US government would be exerted to keep the state from seceding. Although he declined to pass judgment on the actions of Capt. Nathaniel Lyon, Harney did note that no government could be respected that would tolerate the "openly treasonable preparations" that took place at Camp Jackson. He also admitted that there were many loyal, innocent men in the camp. Finally, Harney pledged to protect the people and their property against "all unlawful combinations of men."[5]

Many in Missouri, even pro-Union men, condemned Lyon. Thomas L. Snead, aide to Gov. Claiborne Fox Jackson, believed that "many who till now had never wavered in their fidelity to the Union, [were] now determined to stand with their

WILLIAM S. HARNEY

Born in Tennessee in 1800, Harney was commissioned a second lieutenant in the First Infantry in 1818. He was promoted to first lieutenant in 1819 and to captain in 1825. He served in the Black Hawk War and advanced to major (paymaster) in 1833 and lieutenant colonel of the Second US Dragoons in 1836. He earned a brevet to colonel in 1840 for his actions in the Second Seminole War. In 1846, Harney was promoted to colonel; he participated in Gen. Winfield Scott's Mexico City Campaign in 1847 and brevetted brigadier general of volunteers in 1847 for his performance at the Battle of Cerro Gordo. Harney served on frontier duty in Texas from 1848 to 1854 and led a successful expedition against the Sioux in 1855–1856. He participated in the Third Seminole War, 1856–1857, and the Utah Expedition against the Mormons, 1857–1858. In addition, Harney provided military support to the Kansas territorial government from 1857 to 1858. He was promoted to brigadier general in 1858 and assigned to command the Department of Oregon; during the 1859 "Pig War" controversy with the British on San Juan Island, he commanded the US forces. In 1860, he was replaced as commander of the Department of Oregon, but he took command of the Department of the West the same year. Harney was relieved of command of the Department of the West in April 1861 but was restored to command the following month. A few weeks later, the Lincoln administration lost confidence in Harney and he was relieved of command for the second and final time; Harney did not receive another command and retired from the army in 1863. Brevetted a major general in 1865 for his long and faithful service, Harney was a member of the Southern Treaty Commission and met with the southern plains and other tribes in 1865. He served on the Indian Peace Commission from 1867 to 1869. Harney died on May 9, 1889, in Orlando, Florida.

State, and to resist the government of Abraham Lincoln."[6] Others continued to support the Union cause, reasoning that a military force should not be powerless against a mob merely because it contains women and children. "The place for women and children in such times is at home," wrote one Unionist, and if they choose to be in the presence of armies, "they do it understanding that they risk their lives to gratify their curiosity."[7] One family whose son participated in the capture of the camp cheered the "bold and important" effort aimed at "disarming and disbanding State treason" so that "Missouri will be held to her allegiance."[8]

The events in Saint Louis had a dramatic effect elsewhere in the state. In Jefferson City, state lawmakers already had passed legislation on May 9 giving Governor Jackson ten thousand dollars for "such military service or expenses" as were required and allowing him to keep state militia companies in service for as long as he thought necessary. On the day of the "massacre," Jackson was given another twenty thousand dollars. When word of the events at Camp Jackson reached Jefferson City, the shocked legislature quickly decided that because "citizens of other States had invaded St. Louis" and that a portion of the city was in a state of rebellion, Jackson was authorized to "take such measures as in his judgment he may deem necessary or proper to repel such invasion or put down such rebellion." When the legislature met again at 11:30 p.m., May 10, the members were read a message from Jackson, informing them that two regiments of Federal troops were on their way to the capital. Early the next morning, amid these false rumors, the legislature passed another act giving Jackson a "militia fund" to purchase military supplies and establish an armory. Legislation passed on May 13 and 14 gave the governor the authority to take possession of railroad and telegraph lines and to establish foundries to manufacture arms.

But the most important legislative act, passed on May 14, created the Missouri State Guard. The lengthy act divided the state into nine military districts or divisions and authorized the mobilization of men for suppressing insurrection, repelling invasion, and protecting lives, liberty, or property. Recruits were to swear allegiance to Missouri alone, support the state constitution, and obey the orders of the governor.[9] Armed with

THOMAS L. SNEAD

Born in Henrico County, Virginia, in 1828, Snead graduated from Richmond College in 1846 and the University of Virginia in 1848. He moved to Saint Louis in 1850. Serving as both proprietor and editor in chief of the Saint Louis *Bulletin* in 1860 and 1861, Snead was instrumental in Gov. Claiborne F. Jackson's election.

When the Civil War began, he served as aide-de-camp to Governor Jackson and fought alongside him at the battles of Boonville and Carthage. Appointed chief of ordnance and acting assistant adjutant general in the State Guard in July 1861, Snead served with Sterling Price at Wilson's Creek. He resigned from the State Guard in March 1862, but was commissioned a major in the Confederate Army and served as Price's chief of staff and assistant adjutant general during campaigns in Mississippi and Arkansas. In 1864, Snead represented Missouri in the Confederate Congress.

After the war, he moved to New York City in 1865, serving as editor of the *Daily News* for two years. In 1866, he earned admission to the bar of New York. In 1886 he wrote *The Fight for Missouri*, which chronicled the events in that state from the 1860 election to the Battle of Wilson's Creek. In 1890, Snead died of a heart attack in New York.

this mandate, Governor Jackson appointed former legislator and Mexican War hero Sterling Price as a major general and commander of the State Guard, and Jackson named brigadier generals to command each district. Thousands of Missourians, eager to fight against a dictatorial national government that dared shoot down women and children flocked to organize State Guard companies.

The same day, the legislature also passed a resolution of protest to the "civilized world" against the "unchristian and inhuman violation of our rights" and the murder of defenseless people. Insulted and wronged by an "armed despotism" that hated Missourians, was controlled by no law but passion, and had trampled upon the sacred rights of the people of Missouri, the legislature asked the governor to call the militia to defend the state and "perish, if necessary, in defending their constitutional rights."[10]

Jackson now needed time to organize, arm, and equip his State Guardsmen. If he could craft some sort of temporary truce with the Federals, he could better prepare his militia for the fighting to come. Fortunately for the governor, his counterpart in Saint Louis was once again the older, conservative General Harney rather than the younger, fiery, uncompromising Captain Lyon. Jackson ordered Major General Price to meet with Harney; on May 21, they announced the Price-Harney Agreement, a means of maintaining "the peace of the State, and the defense of the rights and property of all persons, without distinction of party." The agreement quite simply stated that Price would use the power of the state to maintain order; in return, Harney would make no military movements that would disturb the peace. The agreement was to be "most religiously and sacredly kept" and did allow for the "united forces of both Governments" to maintain the peace and defend rights and property and "enforce the terms of the honorable and amicable agreement which has been made."[11]

Despite the promise of peace, the Price-Harney Agreement saw mixed reactions. One contemporary historian wrote that the agreement "was hailed with general approval" and, in fact, was successful.[12] "A Peace Advocate" wrote from Jefferson City that Price's policy, "a peace policy," "has met, and will meet, with the sanction of the great body of the people of the State." Price was an honorable man, the writer continued, who would do nothing to forfeit that esteem and was determined to keep the peace.[13] State Rep. Philip Pipkin believed that "the troubled minds of the people seemed to be calmed, and every man, secessionist or otherwise, settled upon the conviction that peace and quiet would be restored to Missouri."[14]

Radicals such as Col. Francis "Frank" P. Blair saw the agreement as a source of "great disgust and dissatisfaction to the Union men; but I am in hopes we can get along with it."[15] M. Jeff Thompson, a secessionist from Saint Joseph, believed that "we concluded that we were sold and must make the best arrangements to leave the country we could."[16] Secessionist Basil Duke, commander of the Saint Louis "Minute Men," recalled: "This agreement was

STERLING PRICE

Born in Virginia in 1809, Price attended Hampden-Sydney College and studied law; in 1830 he moved with his family to Missouri. He served in the Missouri state legislature; in 1844 he was elected to the US House of Representatives, a position from which he resigned to lead a regiment of Missouri troops in the Mexican War. In 1848 Price was promoted to brigadier general of volunteers. He served as governor of Missouri from 1853 to 1857. He was president of the Missouri convention that voted against secession, but a dispute with radicals prompted his break from the Unionist ranks. Price offered his services to secessionist Gov. Claiborne Fox Jackson and accepted command of the Missouri State Guard. Price worked to maintain peace in Missouri, but after negotiations with Union leaders broke down in June 1861, he prepared his troops to oppose Federal forces; he combined his volunteer forces with those of Brig. Gen. Ben McCulloch's Confederate troops to defeat the Federals at Wilson's Creek, Missouri. Price captured Lexington, Missouri, in September 1861 before retreating into Arkansas. The next year, in March 1862, he led Missouri troops in Maj. Gen. Earl Van Dorn's Confederate force at Elkhorn Tavern, Arkansas; following that defeat, the Missouri troops were mustered into Confederate service and Price was commissioned major general. Price was transferred to Mississippi despite his fervent protest and suffered defeats at Iuka and Corinth before returning to Arkansas. In 1863  he was again defeated at Helena. Price supported Gen. Edmund Kirby Smith in repulsing Gen. Frederick Steele's Arkansas portion of the Red River Campaign in the spring of 1864; that fall he led an ambitious cavalry raid into Missouri, but after initial success, was turned back in eastern Kansas. Retreating through Indian Territory and northern Texas, Price's remnant returned to Arkansas in December 1864. At the close of the war Price refused to surrender and escaped to Mexico; upon the collapse of Maximilian's empire in 1866, Price returned to Missouri, where he died the following year. Called "Old Pap" by his men, Price was a devoted soldier. Although his 1864 raid and subsequent exodus to Mexico have been highly romanticized, his overall military performance was largely unimpressive.

undoubtedly a grave mistake on the part of the Southern men, for the slightest reflection might have convinced them that it was one which would not be maintained."[17]

The *Weekly Missouri Democrat* quickly asserted that Major General Price had entered the agreement "to carry out a treasonable purpose and design" by "secretly arming the State, to overthrow the authority of the general government." Price and Governor Jackson had been "indefatigable" in organizing companies and procuring arms, the newspaper's editor believed, and had sent their men home but told them to be ready for service. "In all parts of the State treason is bold and defiant," he concluded. A resident of Hannibal saw the agreement as "a perfect God-send to the traitors" that lowered the suspicions of Union men and gave the traitors "time and opportunity to work without being watched."[18]

General Harney did not have long to enjoy the fragile peace he had created, and which seemed to appease at least some Missourians. Behind the scenes, Captain Lyon and his supporters, wanting to rid themselves of Harney, had been working since Camp Jackson to have him relieved a second time. On May 16, orders were drafted in Washington sacking the general and granting him a leave of absence "until further orders." President Abraham Lincoln, busy with other affairs, gave Congressman Blair the power to decide when to deliver the order.

Harney's situation did not improve. Within a few days of the general's meeting with Price, Adj. Gen. Lorenzo Thomas advised the department commander of Lincoln's "concern" that, despite the terms of the agreement, reports continued to come in of loyal citizens being driven from their homes. Harney was warned that the "professions of loyalty to the Union" by the state authorities were not to be trusted.

On May 27, Harney told Price that he had received numerous reliable reports of depredations against Union men and offered to form Home Guards at these locations "unless you can give me assurances that such a measure is unnecessary." He hoped that Price would not regard such formations as a violation of their agreement. (Of course, Price believed they would.)[19] Price assured him that all such reports were unfounded. Harney remained optimistic. "Missouri is rapidly becoming tranquillized," he wrote on May 29, and "peace and confidence in the ability of the government to maintain its authority will be fully and permanently restored." "Interference by unauthorized parties," the general believed, could prevent the realization of these hopes. He told his superiors in Washington that he thought the agreement with Price would be carried out in good faith, but he also pledged to watch the state authorities carefully. Any violation of their pledge or attempt at rebellion, he promised, would be "promptly met and put down."

Caught between two fires, with extremists on both sides, and determined to keep peace at all costs, General Harney was doomed. Some, such as contemporary historian Thomas Scharf, believed that Harney was fully prepared to fight if conflict was unavoidable. Others were not certain of that. One thing was certain: Harney "strove to postpone bloodshed as long as possible."[20] On May 30, the general received the order relieving him of command, but the next day he wired Adjutant General Thomas to ask for confirmation, stating he believed that President Lincoln did not want him replaced, and assuring the president that rumors of harassment of Union men were exaggerated and that if he continued in command, "I anticipate no serious disturbance in the State."

The authorities in Washington remained unconvinced. The same day, Captain Lyon announced in general orders that Harney had relinquished command of the department. Along with command of the Department of the West, Lyon also received a brigadier general's commission—a promotion of three ranks—as a reward for his actions in Saint Louis. The stage was now set for a face-to-face confrontation between the two personalities who had helped drive Missouri to the brink of civil war: a newly minted brigadier general and the legally elected governor.

5
"THIS MEANS WAR"

June 1861 began with secessionist and pro-Union Missourians enjoying an uneasy truce under the terms of the Price-Harney Agreement. Within just a few days, however, that period of relative peace would be only a memory.

Several moderates ("well-meaning gentlemen," as Thomas L. Snead labeled them), urged Gov. Claiborne Fox Jackson and Maj. Gen. Sterling Price to meet with Brig. Gen. Nathaniel Lyon in Saint Louis. Lyon was also persuaded to give the two Missourians safe passage to and from Jefferson City "for the purpose of effecting, if possible, a pacific solution of the domestic troubles of Missouri."[1] The Planters' House meeting, the high-stakes effort to save the state from war, took place on June 11. Jackson, his aide Snead, and Price had never met Lyon, but all three had known politician Col. Francis "Frank" P. Blair for years. Yet such familiarity initially bred contempt. Price had not recognized Blair since the former's term as governor, when Blair had used "some very unbecoming language" about Price in a debate in the legislature. To his credit, Blair overcame this initial embarrassment by presenting Price to Lyon with great deference and treating him with consideration, and Price reciprocated. Ironically, the two men resumed a sort of friendship on the very day that they were destined to take up arms against each other.

Fortunately, both sides left their own version of events at the Planters' House, and modern historians can assess what took place that day with some degree of accuracy. A pro-Union newspaper that covered the conference reported that Price insisted that no US troops should be allowed to pass through or be stationed in the state because that would lead to civil war. Instead, the state must remain neutral, he argued, with neither side armed. Governor Jackson offered protection to Union sympathizers but would also disband his State Guard. Lyon replied that if the federal government withdrew its forces, "secret and subtle measures" would be employed to organize forces opposed to the government and drive out loyal citizens—citizens who could not be protected if US troops were banned from Missouri. In addition, a "large aggressive force"—Confederate troops—might move into the state from elsewhere to assist in carrying out "the secession programme," and the state government would be powerless to stop it. Moreover, civil officers could not carry out their duties without the support of military force.

In Lyon's opinion, if the governor would only resist outrages against Union men, repress secessionist activities, call upon or accept assistance from US troops, and allow such soldiers to occupy posts to resist invasion, no infringement of "State rights or dignity" would occur, and peace would be maintained. Jackson proposed that both men begin a correspondence, but Lyon disagreed. He instead proposed that the views of each leader be published, but Jackson disagreed.[2]

Governor Jackson's aide Snead, in a postwar interview, largely agreed with the Union account of the meeting but added certain details. He related that Jackson agreed to disband and disarm the State Guard, repel all Confederate attempts to invade Missouri, and maintain strict neutrality if Lyon would agree to disarm his Home Guards and not occupy any part of the state he did not currently hold. Snead also recalled, however, that Lyon replied that Missouri was part of the Union—it would not be permitted to remain neutral in the national civil war but would have to furnish troops and do whatever else the government required. The authority of the United States, Lyon said, was paramount in Missouri and must be respected. "All this was said slowly, deliberately, coldly and with a peculiar intonation [that] showed that he meant every word that he uttered," Snead remembered.

Clearly, no agreement was possible. Without looking at Major General Price and Governor Jackson, Brigadier General Lyon left the room, his aide Maj. Horace Conant following. Colonel Blair stayed a few moments before he also left. Friends crowded around the Missourians to learn the results of the conference and soon learned that peace was out of the question; Lyon had declared war on the state government.[3]

Jackson and Price left Saint Louis immediately and arrived back in the state capital about two o'clock the following morning. By that time, Jackson had already decided to issue a proclamation mobilizing the Missouri State Guard for service. By daybreak, the proclamation was on its way to the people, and Jackson and several loyal state officers packed official papers and prepared to evacuate the capital. They knew that Lyon and his forces would not be far behind.

Jackson's proclamation informed the people that "wicked and unprincipled men" acting in the name of the US government had inflicted a "series of unprovoked and unparalleled outrages" upon Missouri. Jackson then listed those alleged crimes and noted that, despite the Price-Harney Agreement, the Federals had carried out a "system of hostile operations in utter contempt of that agreement." Despite his efforts at the Planters' House to assure Lyon that he would maintain peace through "a strict neutrality," Governor Jackson's proposal of a series of "humiliating terms" had been rejected, and he had refused Lyon's "degrading terms" as well. Now, faced with "military despotism," Jackson called for fifty thousand volunteers to protect the lives, liberty, and property of Missourians and their "sacred rights and dearest privileges."

Although he told his constituents that Missouri was still in the Union, Jackson also reminded them that "your first allegiance is due to your own State." The same day, General Order No. 11 was issued, ordering all available troops to muster in their respective districts for active service, with the Sixth District's men to assemble at Boonville, west of the capital. Jackson's plan was to abandon pro-Union Jefferson City and consolidate his forces at Boonville, a river town in the midst of friendly territory, where eager recruits from north Missouri could join them.

Many in Missouri realized that the failure of the Planters' House meeting and Jackson's proclamation had officially started the war in Missouri. "With that the die was cast," newspaper editor and Col. Henry Boernstein remembered.[4] The Saint Louis *Weekly Missouri Democrat* wrote that "the Dogs of War" had been unleashed—"Civil war exists in Missouri . . . and the question is now dependent on the power which the respective parties can bring to the contest."[5] An unidentified correspondent in Saint Louis wrote on June 13: "War has begun! The unavoidable conflict, always predicted by me, has at last broken out. . . . The gauntlet has thus been thrown down."[6]

As the governor prepared to lead a government in exile, Lyon read the latest proclamation from Jefferson City and made plans of his own. Regarding Governor Jackson's proclamation as "tantamount to a declaration of war," Brigadier General Lyon proposed to take a portion of his command up the Missouri River to capture Jefferson City and secure the waterway, thereby preventing State Guard units from joining

June 12–14

FORT LEAVENWORTH
Lexington
Boonville
Kansas City
STURGIS
JACKSON
LYON
St. Louis
Jefferson City
Rolla
SIGEL
Carthage
Springfield
Neosho
Cowskin Prairie
Fayetteville

Jackson. At the same time, another Union force would travel by rail down the southwest branch of the Pacific Railroad from Saint Louis to the end of the line at Rolla, then on foot to Springfield, to trap Jackson's forces in the jaws of a giant pincer. On June 13, Lyon's wing left Saint Louis and arrived in Jefferson City two days later, peacefully occupying the capital. The Federals raised the Stars and Stripes on the cupola of the state capitol, and a band played "The Star-Spangled Banner" to the cheers of local Unionists. An unnamed reporter noted that "much disappointment was manifested by the troops on finding that the enemy had fled."[7]

On the same day that Lyon left Saint Louis, Jackson and his followers abandoned the capital and headed for Boonville. There they found a force of only about 450 men, most of them members of the First Rifle Regiment under the command of Jackson's nephew, Col. John Sappington Marmaduke. Although a political appointee, Colonel Marmaduke was no military novice. He had graduated from West Point in 1857 and had served with the Seventh US Infantry, resigning his commission only after President Abraham Lincoln's call for troops. But few of the other Guardsmen had any military experience, and most were armed with shotguns and squirrel rifles rather than military muskets. Even worse, Jackson had temporarily lost his commander in chief. Major General Price had fallen ill after leaving Jefferson City and had returned to his home in nearby Chariton County. But recruits continued to assemble in the Boonville area over the next two days; by June 15, approximately fifteen hundred State Guardsmen had gathered at Camp Bacon, about four miles east of town, ready and eager to face any advancing Federals. A minister "made a speech urging the men to do their duty, telling them they were engaged in a just cause." One captain told his men that "if every one else leaves, I will stay and fight it out by myself."[8]

When word reached him that Governor Jackson's adherents were now concentrated at Boonville, Lyon quickly prepared to leave the capital with 1,700 men to give battle. He explained to Colonel Boernstein that he "could afford to lose no time" and had to strike the camp at Boonville "before this gathering could take on more threatening dimensions."[9] Lyon's force pulled away from the Jefferson City wharf in three boats, to salutes and cheers and a band playing "Hail, Columbia." Much like their State Guard counterparts, the confident Federals were off to take part in the first battle of the war in Missouri. "All our troops are in good health and condition and anxious to meet Claib. Jackson and his bogus 50,000," wrote one reporter. Another correspondent noted that Jackson had often displayed "admirable tact in running," so the Federals were anxious to teach him "a few other and more manly qualities."[10] Newspaper reporter Thomas Knox noticed that the officers and men were "full of enthusiasm," "eagerly anticipating their first encounter" with the rebels, and "wishing an early opportunity for winning glory."[11]

Col. John Sappington Marmaduke, Missouri State Guard.

Lyon had a fairly formidable mixture of US regulars and volunteers. Colonel Blair's First Missouri Infantry and nine companies of Col. Boernstein's Second Missouri were bolstered by Capt. James Totten's Battery F, Second US Artillery, and three companies of regular infantry, including Lyon's own Company B, Second US, and two companies of recruits. Early on the morning of June 17, Lyon disembarked the bulk of his force about eight miles from Boonville. He then marched along the river road, expecting to meet a force of "three or four thousand" of the enemy.

Once again, Jackson had been warned of Lyon's movements. Convinced that a disaster was in the making, Colonel Marmaduke persuaded his uncle to abandon Boonville and concentrate his forces to the southwest at Warsaw. By the next morning, however, two or three officers had talked Jackson into making a stand at Boonville. Marmaduke protested and even offered his resignation, but Jackson assured him that he would bear responsibility for what would occur. Many years later, Jackson's aide Thomas Snead explained that the governor fought at Boonville to buy time for reinforcements to arrive, to allow civilians to evacuate the

JAMES TOTTEN

Born in Pennsylvania in 1818, Totten graduated twenty-fifth of fifty-two at the US Military Academy in 1841. Commissioned a brevet second lieutenant of artillery upon graduation, Totten was promoted to second lieutenant the following year. He served at various posts through the 1850s and was promoted to captain in 1855. In 1860 he assumed command of

the federal arsenal at Little Rock, Arkansas, and was forced to surrender the post to a superior force of Arkansas militia the following February; allowed to evacuate Little Rock, he moved to Saint Louis and assisted with the capture of Missouri State Militia forces at Camp Jackson in May 1861; as part of the Army of the West under the command of Brig. Gen. Nathaniel Lyon, he led Battery F, Second US Artillery, in the occupation of the Missouri capital at Jefferson City and at the Battle of Boonville, Missouri, in June 1861, and was promoted to brevet major for the latter action. For his important service at Wilson's Creek, Totten was promoted to brevet lieutenant colonel; Maj. Samuel Sturgis, who took command of the army following Brigadier General Lyon's death, believed that Totten should be a household name. After various staff assignments, Totten was named a brigadier general in the Missouri State Militia in February 1862; he led a division in the Army of the Frontier, and after further staff duty, participated in the Siege of Mobile in March–April 1865. He was brevetted a brigadier general for gallant and meritorious services during the war. Totten continued in the Regular Army, but hampered by alcoholism, was dismissed in 1870 for disobedience of orders and neglect of duty. Totten died in Sedalia, Missouri, in October 1871.

town, and to let State Guard officers destroy military stores and the state armory and workshop that had been moved from Jefferson City. Reassured by Jackson, Marmaduke reluctantly but dutifully marched about five hundred of his green soldiers east out of Camp Bacon to meet the Federals.

Brigadier General Lyon's men had moved only about two miles before they encountered the first State Guard skirmishers. The Missourians made a brief stand—what Lyon described as "a weak effort"—and then fell back, intending to draw the Federals into their "stronghold." Lyon marched on another mile and encountered the main body of Guardsmen. Marmaduke's forces put up more of a fight here and even "held on with considerable resolution, and gave us a check for a short time and made some havoc."[12] But the better-trained and better-equipped Union troops, especially Captain Totten's battery, poured fire on the enemy.

Governor Jackson himself ordered his men to withdraw, but some resolute

Missouri State Guardsmen P. S. Alexander (right), a member of the Moniteau County Rangers, and S. W. Stone of the California (MO) Guards, taken in Jefferson City in May 1861.

Missourians soon halted, formed a new line of battle, and advanced again against the Federals. It was only a temporary rally, and the enemy's discipline soon broke the Missouri line and routed Jackson's men, who retreated to the camp and the town and across the Missouri River. The State Guard camp fell into Union hands, along with two iron guns, some tents, small arms, ammunition, two flags, and about sixty prisoners. By 11:00 a.m., Lyon had accepted the town's surrender. The skirmish had lasted twenty to thirty minutes but had cost few casualties. The Federals had two killed, one missing, and nine wounded (two of the wounded subsequently died), and the Missouri forces suffered only a handful of losses as well. The disgusted Colonel Marmaduke resigned his commission after all and went south to join the Confederate Army. As his dejected troops marched to the southwest, away from Lyon and

June 15–17

FORT LEAVENWORTH

Lexington

STURGIS Kansas City

Boonville

JACKSON LYON

St. Louis

Jefferson City *Captured June 15*

Rolla

SIGEL

Carthage

Springfield

Neosho

Cowskin Prairie

Fayetteville

his victorious Federals, Jackson made a quick side trip to his home in nearby Arrow Rock. After grabbing his personal papers, he too went south to catch his retreating State Guardsmen.

Although only a minor skirmish, the "Boonville Races" had a far-reaching impact. To the Federals, it was a great victory. "Let the lion roar!" shouted the *Chicago Tribune*, noting Brigadier General Lyon's "eminent fitness" for command and the fact that "the valiant little brigadier" had shown "Napoleonic promptness" in dealing with the secessionists.[13] One political cartoon, titled "The Battle of Booneville, or the Great Missouri 'Lyon' Hunt," showed the brigadier general in the form of a lion. Another, captioned "Strayed," depicted Governor Jackson as an ass who had run away from Boonville after being frightened by a "lion." The defeat dealt a "stunning blow to the Southern-rights men of Missouri," Jackson's aide Snead confessed, and was "the most brilliant achievement of Lyon's well-conceived campaign." Whereas Camp Jackson had completed the "conquest" of Saint Louis, Snead argued, Lyon's capture of Jefferson City had robbed the governor of the "prestige which sustains established and acknowledged authority." It made the Missouri River "a Federal highway," deprived Jackson of recruits from north Missouri, and drove him from a sympathetic region of the state.[14] Jackson's State Guard had clearly lost its first encounter with the Federals, but the troops would have several more opportunities to redeem themselves before the end of the campaign.

6

SWEENY AND SIGEL

As Brig. Gen. Nathaniel Lyon routed the State Guard at
Boonville, the other jaw of his giant pincer was making prog-
ress as well. Capt. Thomas W. Sweeny, an old regular in Lyon's
Second US Infantry, commanded the troops heading from Saint
Louis into southwest Missouri. Although Sweeny was forced to
remain in the city arranging supplies, Col. Franz Sigel and the
Third Missouri Infantry left Saint Louis by train on June 13.
Sigel arrived the next day in Rolla, where, as Lyon had done at
the state capital, the Federals raised the Stars and Stripes and
established Union authority. But at Rolla the rail line ended,
and the Union volunteers were forced to march on foot the rest
of the 110-mile journey to Springfield.

Despite the difficulty of moving over a poor road through
rough country, Sigel continued his triumphal march into southwest Missouri. On June 17, he left Rolla with his own Third
Missouri, four companies of the Fifth Missouri Infantry, and
Franz Backoff's Artillery Battalion (two batteries, or eight

THOMAS WILLIAM SWEENY

Born in 1820 in Ireland, Sweeny came to the United States in 1832 and apprenticed to a publishing house. At the start of the Mexican War, he was elected second lieutenant in Company A, First New York Volunteers. He joined Gen. Winfield Scott's army at Vera Cruz and was badly wounded at the Battle of Churubusco, August 20, 1847, which required the amputation of his right arm. Sweeny was appointed second lieutenant in the Second Infantry in 1848. He sailed with his regiment from New York to Monterey, California, arriving in April 1849, and helped establish Fort Yuma in 1850. He was promoted to first lieutenant in 1851 and engaged in the Yuma Indian War in 1852, where he received a severe arrow wound. He was ordered to Fort Pierre, Nebraska Territory, in 1854 and served as aide to Gen. William S. Harney during the Sioux Expedition of 1855–1856. Sweeny participated in the Spirit Lake Expedition in Minnesota in 1857 and was ordered to New York on recruiting duty in 1858. He was promoted to captain in January 1861 and ordered to the Federal arsenal at Saint Louis. Sweeny assisted Capt. Nathaniel Lyon with the defense of the arsenal and mustering of US volunteers; then

guns). At Lebanon, Sigel's men were presented with a beautiful bouquet as the Union band played "Hail, Columbia." A ladies singing society performed "The Star-Spangled Banner." Even more inspiring to Sigel was the news that Lyon had won at Boonville and that the State Guard was retreating south with Lyon in pursuit.

After a disagreeable thirty-six-hour-march through rain, the vanguard of Colonel Sigel's Germans arrived in Springfield on June 23. They entered the largest town in southwest Missouri with a band playing national airs and a welcome from young ladies wearing the national colors. Because a majority of Springfield's residents were pro-Union, Sigel's reception was friendly. One soldier contentedly wrote, "The citizens here are doing their best to show their patriotism. Anything in their power we can get without money." But there was also a he participated in the capture of the Missouri State Militia at Camp Jackson in May 1861. Sweeny was elected brigadier general by members of the US Reserve Corps in Saint Louis and then ordered to Springfield, Missouri, where he arrived July 1. He led an expedition to Forsyth, Missouri, and fought a skirmish there with Missouri State Guard forces. He served as inspector general of the Army of the West on the staff of, by then a brigadier general, Nathaniel Lyon and participated in the Battle of Wilson's Creek, where he was wounded. Sweeny accepted the colonelcy of the Fifty-second Illinois Infantry in January 1862 and led a brigade in W. H. L. Wallace's Division at the Battle of Shiloh, where he was again wounded. Sweeny took command of his brigade at the Battle of Corinth, October 3–4, 1862, when his superior officer was mortally wounded. He was commissioned a brigadier general of volunteers the following month, and his brigade performed garrison duty and protected the Memphis and Charleston Railroad in 1863. Sweeny was given command of a division in the fall of 1863 and led it during the Atlanta Campaign, participating in the Battle of Atlanta and other actions. Sweeny was placed under arrest after fisticuffs with his superior in July 1864; he was court-martialed but acquitted. In August 1865, he was mustered out of the volunteer service and dismissed from the Regular Army in December 1865. In 1866 Sweeny assumed command of the Fenian (Irish Revolutionary) Army that invaded Canada; after that army withdrew from Canada, Sweeny was restored to his rank in the Regular Army and retired in 1870. He died on Long Island on April 10, 1892.

secessionist element in Springfield, so Sigel surrounded the town and seized about fifty secessionist civilians, including Rev. Charles Carleton and the men of his congregation.

Word reached Sigel in Springfield that Gov. Claiborne Jackson and his State Guard were moving toward the town of Lamar, approximately sixty miles northwest of Springfield. The impetuous Sigel—an observer described him as "quick to decide and prompt to act"[1]—left a garrison in Springfield and began to push his men west on the evening of June 25 to "try to catch the fox."[2] At the town of Sarcoxie on June 28, Sigel learned that seven or eight hundred men under Maj. Gen. Sterling Price were camped near Neosho, awaiting Confederate reinforcements from Arkansas before moving north to meet the governor. Knowing he was now between two enemy forces, the German colonel resolved to attack Price and then turn on Jackson.

But after Colonel Sigel left Sarcoxie on the morning of June 29, he learned that the troops camped near Neosho had fled. Now he turned his attention to the northern column. Sigel remained at Neosho for the first three days in July, sending detachments and scouting parties out in different directions to find the enemy. Finally, on July 4, "after paying due honors to the day of American Independence" by parading and firing a national salute, Sigel took his remaining 1,100 men and eight guns to Carthage.[3] He left behind a company as a garrison for Neosho. The march to Carthage was hot and dusty, but the Germans reached the city that night and camped southeast of the town square.

The Greene County Courthouse in Springfield sketched by artist Alexander Simplot in the fall of 1861. The building was used as a hospital before and after Wilson's Creek.

After the defeat at Boonville, Governor Jackson's State Guard had steadily moved toward southwest Missouri. The governor himself had caught up with his retreating troops at Syracuse. In the meantime, Major General Price had left his sickbed and arrived on June 18 in Lexington on the Missouri River. Although he found about two thousand State Guardsmen waiting there, he soon learned of the disaster at Boonville. Boxed in on the west by enemy troops from Fort Leavenworth and Kansas City, and on the east by Brigadier General Lyon, Price ordered Gen. James S. Rains to assume command of the men at Lexington and start them moving south to join Jackson at Lamar. Price would also head southwest, but with only a small escort. His mission was to make contact with Confederate forces in Arkansas and find help to reclaim Missouri.

Governor Jackson pushed his troops hard to the town of Warsaw and then across the Osage River, putting a natural barrier between his forces and Lyon's. There he learned of

July 1

FORT LEAVENWORTH

Lexington

Kansas City

STURGIS

Boonville

LYON

St. Louis

Jefferson City

Rolla

JACKSON

SIGEL

Carthage

Springfield

Neosho

Cowskin Prairie

McCULLOCH

Fayetteville

Price's mission and General Rains's movement. Jackson's men trudged into Camp Lamar, three miles north of that town, and Rains joined him there on July 3. They were headed directly toward a confrontation with Colonel Sigel's German volunteers.

On the night of July 4, State Guard foragers collided with Sigel's pickets but withdrew after a brief skirmish. Jackson now faced an enemy of unknown strength blocking his retreat route and the avenue of approach for any Confederate help from Arkansas. With four thousand armed men, and an estimated two thousand without weapons, Jackson decided to move south toward Carthage the following morning and strike

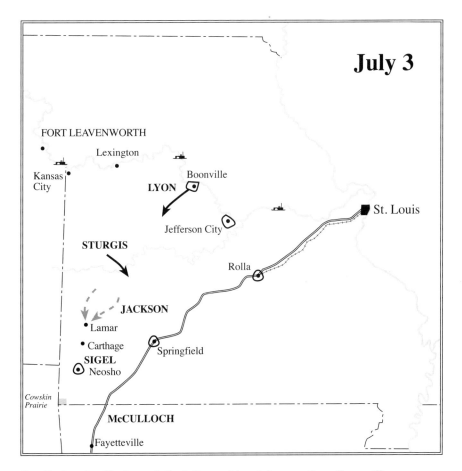

July 3

FORT LEAVENWORTH

Lexington

Kansas City

Boonville

LYON

St. Louis

Jefferson City

STURGIS

Rolla

JACKSON

Lamar

Carthage

Springfield

SIGEL

Neosho

Cowskin Prairie

McCULLOCH

Fayetteville

the Federals. He hoped that it would not be another Boonville. Sigel had the same idea; rather than wait for Jackson to find him, he would march north the next day and bring the State Guard to battle.

About 7:00 a.m. on July 5, Governor Jackson's scouts caught sight of Colonel Sigel's column about ten miles north of Carthage. The Federals had crossed a series of parallel rivers and streams—Spring River, Buck Branch Creek, Dry Fork Creek, and Double Trouble Creek—as they marched north from Carthage. About 9:00 a.m., Sigel found the superior State Guard enemy deployed along a slight ridge just north of Double

FRANZ SIGEL

Born in the Grand Duchy of Baden (Germany) in 1824, Sigel graduated from the military academy at Karlsrule in 1843 and served as a lieutenant in the service of Grand Duke Leopold; he fled Germany after his participation in the failed Revolution of 1848. After stays in Switzerland and England, Sigel made his way to the United States in 1852; settling in New York, he taught school and held a commission in the New York Militia. Moving to Saint Louis, Missouri, he became director of schools and a leader in the large German community there; at the outbreak of the Civil War he offered his services to the Union and was appointed colonel of the Third Missouri Infantry and, shortly thereafter, brigadier general of volunteers. He participated in the capture of Camp Jackson and at Wilson's Creek in 1861; he commanded a division and played a conspicuous role in the Battle of Pea Ridge in March 1862. After being promoted to major general, Sigel transferred to the Eastern Theater, where he led a division in the Shenandoah Valley; he commanded the First Corps, Army of Virginia, during the Second Bull Run Campaign of 1862. Thereafter, he directed the Eleventh Corps, Army of the Potomac, from September 1862 through February 1863, but he saw little action and was forced to relinquish corps command due to poor health. Returning to duty in March 1864, Sigel assumed command of the Department of West Virginia; in May 1864, Sigel's command was routed at New Market, Virginia, by Gen. John C. Breckinridge's Confederate force that included a contingent of cadets from the Virginia Military Institute. Relieved of departmental command, Sigel took charge of the Reserve Division, Department of West Virginia, but saw little action for the rest of the war. He resigned his commission in May 1865. After the war, he became active in Democratic politics and ran for numerous offices, eventually becoming a US pension agent in New York by appointment of President Grover Cleveland. Sigel died in New York City in 1902. Although his New Market defeat destroyed his military reputation, General Sigel deserved much credit for rallying thousands of German immigrants to the Union cause; "I fights mit Sigel" became a proud exclamation of German-born soldiers throughout the Federal army.

Trouble Creek. The State Guard formed "a dark line against the azure skies of the horizon, and three banners gaily floating over the line," remembered Union volunteer Sgt. Otto C. Lademann.

Lt. William Barlow, a State Guard artilleryman, wrote that he looked down from the ridge and saw "the bright guns of the federal battery and their finely uniformed infantry deploying on the green prairie." Jackson's aide Thomas L. Snead was also impressed with Sigel's men, recalling that the enemy deployed "with the precision of veterans."[4] But despite the impressive appearance of the Germans, the State Guardsmen were confident of success. With seven guns and a strong force of infantry in line of battle and cavalry in position on both flanks, Jackson's army appeared formidable. But rather than retreat in the face of a superior enemy, the Federal commander formed his line of battle and began to advance across open ground.

Just before 10:00 a.m., with only about eight hundred yards separating the two sides, Sigel ordered his artillery commander to open fire. "Our German gunners were anxious to get into action and instill respect in the rebels," wrote one participant.[5] Jackson's guns "answered promptly." State Guardsman John P. Bell remembered these opening moments of his first taste of combat years later: "We were ordered to lie down. . . . To have seen those cannon balls rolling and bouncing through the grass as they sought the hilltop is a memory we cannot forget."[6] Lieutenant Barlow remembered the roar of shot and bursting of shell, men exhausted by excitement and the heat, wild artillery mules, and prayers that the enemy would run and bring the fight to an end.[7] Accounts differ as to the duration of the bombardment; estimates range from twenty minutes to nearly an hour. The artillery duel "made a great deal of noise but really did very little harm," one participant admitted.[8]

However long it was, the State Guard commanders had had enough of the bombardment. On the Southern right, General Rains led his mounted forces forward either to outflank the Federals or to capture their artillery. At the same time, independent of Rains, Gen. M. M. Parsons thought of the same maneuver on the opposite end of the State Guard line. Gradually, State Guard cavalrymen began to move around both Federal flanks.

Colonel Sigel for a brief moment contemplated an assault on the State Guard line on the ridge, but when informed by one of his battery commanders that he was low on ammunition and could not support the attack, and with enemy cavalrymen moving around both flanks, he opted for retreat. "With great mortification," the Federal colonel began to retire south toward Dry Fork Creek, dividing his command into two sections—one to defend his large number of baggage and supply wagons and the other to act as a rear guard to hold the creek crossing.

The Federals made a resolute stand at the highly defensible Dry Fork ford. Vigorous State Guard infantry attacks could not carry the position, and the heavy fighting there accounted for most of the casualties in the battle. Finally, about 1:00 p.m., the enemy once again worked beyond Sigel's flanks, and he resumed his retreat. Unfortunately for the Germans, some State Guard cavalrymen had moved to block his withdrawal at Buck Branch, the next crossing. Just when it seemed as if Sigel's luck had run out—it appeared that the State Guard cavalry would simply hold the Federals in place until their comrades moved on them from the north—a Federal bayonet charge cleared the ford and reopened Sigel's escape route.

Colonel Sigel made his final defensive stand before reentering Carthage about a half mile north of Spring River. But the disorganized and exhausted State Guardsmen did not initially pose a great threat, and about 6:00 p.m., Sigel successfully shifted his troops and wagon train across the river and began moving the final mile back into Carthage. Although the Federal colonel had hoped finally to give his men a rest in the town square, Governor Jackson's men, refreshed and reorganized, crossed Spring River and began to close in on three sides of the square. Once again, Sigel was forced to fall back, this time fighting through the streets of Carthage. The determined State Guardsmen launched a final unsuccessful attack about 9:00 p.m. on Sigel's rear guard east of town. But darkness put an end to the fighting; the Federals safely retreated to the southeast, on to Sarcoxie, and eventually, several days later, back to Springfield.

Jackson's exhausted men rested in Carthage, unable to continue the pursuit. "We returned to a house on the edge of town," wrote Missourian Henry Cheavens, "and, getting a bite to eat, lay on the floor, covered with blood, dust, and sweat. My feelings then were strange, yet I slept soundly."[9] State Guardsman Bell recalled that of the four companies in his command that had started the fight in the morning, no more than twenty men were still in the ranks when the battle ended. In Bell's company, only three were left—the rest, if not dead or wounded, "were prostrated and fell by the roadside,

BENJAMIN McCULLOCH

Born in Tennessee in 1811, McCulloch followed his friend and neighbor, David Crockett, to Texas in 1835. Unable to reach San Antonio before the fall of the Alamo, McCulloch served under Sam Houston in the Battle of San Jacinto; remaining in Texas, he worked as a surveyor and embarked on a brilliant career as a Texas Ranger, Indian fighter, and scout. In 1839 he was elected to the Republic of Texas House of Representatives but served only a single two-year term. During the

Mexican War, he served with great distinction under Zachary Taylor and gained a national reputation as commander of a Ranger company and Taylor's chief of scouts. During the 1849 Gold Rush, McCulloch ventured to California; failing to find his fortune, he returned to Texas. He was considered for the colonelcy of the newly constituted Second US Cavalry, the command of which went to his fellow Texan Albert Sidney Johnston. In 1854 McCulloch became a US marshal in Texas and in 1858 helped negotiate a settlement between the Mormons and the federal government. With the secession of Texas, McCulloch became a colonel of Texas state troops and secured the surrender of the Federal garrison at San Antonio; in May 1861 he was commissioned a brigadier general in the Confederate army and given command of the Indian Territory. Assigned to command Confederate troops in Arkansas, he defeated Brig. Gen. Nathaniel Lyon's Federal forces at Wilson's Creek, Missouri. A continuing feud with Missouri major general Sterling Price forced the Confederate government to place McCulloch and Price under the command of Maj. Gen. Earl Van Dorn. In March 1862 McCulloch was killed while commanding the right wing in the Battle of Pea Ridge. His death was considered a major blow to Confederate aspirations in the Trans-Mississippi Theater. His brother, Henry E. McCulloch, also served the Confederacy as a brigadier general.

while big, strong, muscular young men could not keep the pace Sigel set us."[10]

Bell wrote that the pursuit of Sigel into Carthage had been "a helter-skelter race" with "every man for himself."[11] Despite the intense fighting, casualties were relatively light. Only about seventy-five State Guardsmen were killed, wounded, or missing, and Sigel lost just over half that number. Although the Battle of Carthage was quickly eclipsed by later, far more intense battles and "hardly rose to the dignity of a respectable skirmish," according to one veteran, the fight was a difficult, physically exhausting, twelve-hour running battle in intense July heat.[12] Both sides had been pushed to physical exhaustion.

Colonel Sigel's small group of soldiers had saved themselves from destruction, had fought with "the greatest skill and bravery," and no doubt "stood like veterans, and defended one position after the other without one man leaving the ranks" against a far superior enemy. On the other hand, if their commander had carefully considered his predicament and shown more wisdom, perhaps the Saint Louis Germans would not have been required to demonstrate such bravery.[13]

The fortunes of war had smiled on the Federals in another way. At Major General Price's urging, a large force of Confederates under Brig. Gen. Benjamin McCulloch had crossed the Missouri-Arkansas line on a forced march to assist Governor Jackson and had, in fact, captured the company that Sigel had left at Neosho without firing a shot. Sergeant Lademann, a member of the Third Missouri and one of Sigel's harshest critics, asserted that "we ought never to have left" Springfield and reasoned that if McCulloch had been able to reach Jackson's forces in time, the Germans "would have been caught like rats in a trap."[14] But because of his "victory" at Carthage, Sigel was seen as a great hero by the Northern press. The *Weekly Missouri Democrat* proclaimed that the German had no equal in the volunteer ranks. His retreat at Carthage "was one of the most masterly military maneuvers" thus far in the war, and "a more admirable display of military science has never been witnessed in this country." The newspaper placed Sigel "in the front ranks of the military men of the day." "We challenge anything in the history of the wars of this country that will surpass this masterly retreat."[15] Although Sigel was always a popular leader in Saint Louis, even New

JOHN TAYLOR HUGHES

Born in Kentucky in 1817, Hughes moved to Howard County, Missouri, in 1820; he entered Bonne Femme College in 1840 and graduated in 1844. He was teaching school at Liberty, Missouri, when the Mexican War began and he enlisted as a private in Company C, First Regiment Missouri Mounted Volunteers, under Col. Alexander Doniphan. Hughes marched with Doniphan's regiment from Fort Leavenworth to Santa Fe and El Paso, and through northern Mexico to

Matamoros, before returning to Saint Louis, having traveled some 5,500 miles in twelve months. Hughes became the unofficial historian of the Doniphan campaign as the author of the book *Doniphan's Expedition*, published in 1848, which made him one of the best known men in Missouri. Hughes was appointed receiver of the US Land Office in Plattsburg, Missouri, in 1849 and elected as a Whig to the Missouri House of Representatives in 1854; he was engaged in many business ventures including a large farm and commercial business buildings. Although Hughes advocated that Missouri remain in the Union in the spring of 1861, he joined the Missouri State Guard as captain of Company K, First Infantry Regiment, Fourth Division, in May 1861; he was elected colonel the following month and participated in the Battle of Carthage. At the Battle of Wilson's Creek his regiment and an attached battalion suffered severely, losing 36 killed, 30 missing, and 76 wounded out of about 650 men engaged. He participated in the Siege of Lexington in September 1861 and then was placed in command of a battalion of Missouri Confederate troops; at the Battle of Pea Ridge, March 7–8, 1862, his battalion served in the Second Missouri Brigade and suffered light casualties in the fighting around Elkhorn Tavern. Hughes went with Maj. Gen. Sterling Price and the Missouri Confederate forces to Mississippi. In the summer of 1862, Hughes returned to Missouri, supposedly as a brevet brigadier general, to recruit troops. He directed the successful Confederate attack on the Union garrison of Independence, Missouri, on August 11, 1862, and was killed at the conclusion of the action. Hughes was respected as a combat commander by troops on both sides.

York newspapers took notice of the new hero; some troops with Brigadier General Lyon believed that Sigel's "brilliant achievement of the 5th entitles him to a much higher consideration than he will be apt to receive."[16]

On the other side of the battlefield, the Missouri State Guard had redeemed itself after the Boonville Races. The raw troops had fought well, earned valuable combat experience, and passed their first test as a true army by scoring a clear victory. State Guard Col. John Taylor Hughes proudly wrote that his men "stood the fire like veterans" and "bore themselves gallantly."[17] Many probably agreed with Lieutenant Barlow that, at the time, Carthage was thought of as "a great battle and a great victory."[18] But like Colonel Sigel, the overall State Guard commander may be faulted as well. Although Governor Jackson was nominally in command and had the distinction of being the only sitting governor to lead troops in battle during the Civil War, he apparently gave few commands on the field of Carthage. A number of other State Guard officers made largely independent decisions instead, and the lack of a unified State Guard command may have contributed greatly to Sigel's salvation on July 5. In the words of Colonel Hughes, "A vigorous concerted effort of the infantry and cavalry would have captured the entire army."[19] Even though the Federal force had escaped annihilation, Jackson and his men were safe from pursuit and now had a clear route open to far southwestern Missouri, where Major General Price waited and Confederate allies were conveniently camped just across the border in Arkansas. "Jackson and his troops did, indeed, have abundant cause to rejoice," wrote Jackson's aide Snead, "for, though we had not won a great victory as we foolishly fancied, or established the independence of the Confederacy as some believed, we had escaped a very great danger."[20] Now, wrote one optimistic Missouri officer, the "government of Missouri must be re-established, and the liberties of the people restored. When we return, this is our motto: 'We come to deliver you.'"[21]

7
LYON'S FORCED MARCH

Although Brig. Gen. Nathaniel Lyon had hoped to act in concert with Capt. Thomas Sweeny and Col. Franz Sigel and close the jaws of his trap soon after the victory at Boonville, bad luck finally visited the Federal commander.

Whereas Sweeny had been able to move troops quickly via the railroad from Saint Louis to Rolla, and Lyon himself had been able to transport troops with relative ease up the Missouri River to Boonville, the area between Boonville and Springfield was void of navigable rivers or railroads. Lyon would need supplies and reinforcements to march the 150 miles south from Boonville to Springfield and then defeat the numerically superior State Guard army.

Lyon had hoped to leave Boonville by June 26, but various problems delayed the army's departure. Wagons were in short supply; mules and horses had to be broken; supplies had to be assembled; and rain continued for days, turning roads into quagmires. Lyon himself worked tirelessly to prepare his

force for the upcoming campaign. "He is the hardest working man in the camp," wrote one reporter, being "General,
Quartermaster, Commissary, Commander of the fleet, and I
came nearly [to] saying cook, for the whole army." Brigadier
General Lyon also answered correspondence and dealt with
complaints and requests from officers and civilians "and a
hundred other trifling matters." Civilians in the area enjoyed
a "golden harvest" as the general bought all the mules,
horses, and wagons he could, even though they were "unwor-
thy of Uncle Sam," with a great portion of the animals "rickety, starved and broken down."[1]

"We have had a bustling time preparing for the march,"
wrote one Federal soldier. "Horses and wagons, and stores of
all the various munitions of war fill the camp."[2] "Preparations
are neither few nor small," reported one correspondent. More
than 150 wagons (each pulled by two to ten horses or mules)
were needed, plus saddle horses, "making in all a drove of
some five or six hundred draught and saddle animals." A committee of three officers and two citizens was kept busy apprais-
ing the value of civilian horses and wagons and paying for them
by draft because Lyon thought it best not to hire them but to
purchase them.[3]

But no matter how many wagons, horses, and mules he
accumulated, Lyon still needed clear weather and more men
to make his campaign a reality. Correspondent Franc Wilkie
noted that "we have had sprinklings, little showers, heavy
rains every day since our arrival, and in addition to all these
we have had several rainy days—days when it rained all day
and night and the day following and the next day and then sat
in for a rainy day." The rain was so intense that the whole
county was covered in mud ranging from twelve inches to
three feet in depth.[4]

On the other hand, Lyon did receive welcome reinforcements: the nine hundred-man First Iowa Infantry. The Iowans
presented a less than martial appearance, and Lyon was said

to have been "greatly disappointed" with their "varied and poor uniform, many of the men being fairly ragged." Only one company in the regiment carried modern rifle muskets. But the Iowans were anxious for a fight, and with Union troops committed to hold a number of important points in the state, the Federal commander was no doubt glad to have any reinforcements at all.[5]

Finally, on the morning of July 3, with the showers at an end, Lyon's 2,350 men and his hastily assembled supply train left Boonville to the cheers of local citizens who presented bouquets of red, white, and blue flowers to the general and several of his officers. The next day, the column "celebrated" the national day of independence by "cursing the heat, the dust, Claib. Jackson, and things generally," without any firing, toasts, or speeches.[6] Four days of steady marching brought the Federals to the town of Clinton on the Grand River. There they joined a force of 2,200 US regulars and Kansas volunteers under the command of Maj. Samuel Sturgis. The Kansans had joined the regulars at Fort Leavenworth and then marched on to Kansas City. They had intended to help trap Gov. Claiborne Fox Jackson during his retreat, but they were delayed in crossing the Grand River by the same heavy rains that had afflicted Lyon.

The bridges across the river had been burned, so a tedious, laborious crossing of the Grand River on a single boat (a "small scow" or "a "rickety old ferry boat," as some described it) began on the afternoon of July 7. Finally across, Brigadier General Lyon's advance reached the next major obstacle, the Osage River, at about noon on July 9. As the army crossed the Osage, word arrived in the Federal camp that Colonel Sigel's force was retreating to Springfield, pursued by Governor Jackson, and would soon be surrounded and destroyed. The faulty intelligence caused intense excitement and prompted Lyon to send his eager troops toward Springfield on a rapid forced march. They started their epic journey at 5:00 a.m. July 11.

"We had a hot Southern sun to march under, but we kept on with but very few failing," wrote Iowan Ralph Zublin. "The dust and heat were oppressive. Along the roadside were strewed by scores the regulars, as we call the United States troops and the Missouri volunteers." After making twenty-seven miles, the men halted at 3:00 p.m. to eat and rest. After a brief rest, perhaps three hours, the march began again. Rough roads, steep hills, mud, thick forests, swift streams, rocks, and stumps made marching difficult. "I carried myself along more asleep than awake," Zublin complained. Mounted men had to dismount and lead their horses to avoid falling from their saddles

asleep. Others dropped in their tracks and, despite threats
of punishment, refused to move and were left where they fell.
About 3:00 a.m. July 12, after marching forty-eight miles, the
men—"shivering, sleepy and hungry"—were allowed to rest in
a muddy, dew-covered cornfield. After a reprieve of only two
hours, the exhausted Federals were ready to start again, but
luckily, after a march of five more miles, a messenger arrived
just after daylight and announced that Sigel's force was safe.[7]

On the evening of July 13, Lyon rode into Springfield
"mounted on an iron-gray horse," with "an escort or body-
guard of ten men," all of whom were "remarkable for their

large size, strong physique, and fine horsemanship."[8] The
Federal commander immediately went to work acquiring animals and food from the locals, assessing the strategic situation
with his subordinates Captain Sweeny and Colonel Sigel, issu-
ing commissions to Home Guard officers, and mustering their
units. The day after his arrival, he held a formal inspection of
his troops.

But the aggressive commander was "in a 'peck'—better perhaps a bushel—of troubles," as one correspondent wrote, and
he knew it.[9] His troops were relatively few in number, were
far from their supply base, and were threadbare and hungry
after the arduous campaign. Lyon fired off dispatches asking
for help. One went to Saint Louis and Col. Chester Harding, his
quartermaster at the arsenal, pleading for clothing—particularly shoes, shirts, and coats—"in considerable quantities" for
his needy troops. The other dispatch went to Adj. Gen. Lorenzo
Thomas in Washington, also asking for supplies and clothing
and advising him that Governor Jackson would soon have thirty
thousand men. Lyon needed ten thousand more, he argued, or
he would be forced to abandon his position.[10]

Even though Brigadier General Lyon's supply situation
grew more critical with each passing day, he was not content to sit in Springfield and simply complain to his superiors. When word arrived of a State Guard marshaling area
and a supply depot at Forsyth, about fifty miles southeast
of Springfield, Lyon ordered Captain Sweeny to take five
hundred men (six companies) of the First Iowa, the Second
Kansas Infantry, two companies of regular cavalry, and Lt.
George Sokalski's section of US artillery—in all, 1,200 men—
to break up the State Guard camp. Once again, the Federals
suffered through the heat and dust and, when they stopped
to camp that night, endured the obligatory thunderstorm, "as
if the Indian Ocean had been upset on us," reporter Wilkie
wrote. The column marched on the next day through the rain
and camped that night.

On the following afternoon, July 22, the Federals approached Forsyth. They charged on the double quick and with a yell the last three miles into town. About seventy-five State Guardsmen put up a brief fight (Pvt. Eugene F. Ware of Iowa wrote that "there was some shooting—not much") but soon retreated. Their first skirmish impressed all of Captain Sweeny's command. "The effect of the booming of the cannon, the crashing of the bombs and canister and grape through the trees over our heads," wrote one Federal, "the falling branches, and the constant and rapid discharge of small arms . . . we will none of us soon forget," but "the boys all stood firm."[11]

First Sgt. Arthur Gunther (*right*, wearing overcoat), a resident of Lawrence, Kansas, served with Company D, Second Kansas Infantry at Wilson's Creek.

Reporter Wilkie went to investigate the county courthouse in the center of town, where he found clothing and rifles abandoned by the State Guardsmen. Unknown to the correspondent, Sweeny, overlooking the town, had ordered Sokalski's artillery to be brought to bear on Forsyth. Lieutenant Sokalski apparently misunderstood his commander, as he not only unlimbered his howitzer but also commenced firing, sending three artillery rounds through the courthouse. Wilkie narrowly avoided being killed and left the building with a severe head wound from which "the blood ran in streams." In about an hour, Forsyth was secure, and Sweeny's Federals had scored a victory.

In Forsyth, the Federals captured three prisoners and a large amount of food and military supplies. They lost a few horses and had three men (including Wilkie) wounded. Wilkie estimated State Guard losses at five killed and thirteen wounded, but he probably exaggerated the damage done by his comrades.[12] The men of Sweeny's Forsyth expedition were disappointed by the short duration of the fighting, but they were proud of their accomplishment, for they had demonstrated that they were not "holiday soldiers." Very soon they would all experience a much longer and far more deadly encounter with the enemy.[13]

The victorious Federals returned to Springfield on July 25. There any euphoria about Forsyth must have quickly faded.

News of the Federal disaster at the Battle of Bull Run, rumors that a superior force of the enemy was gathering to the southwest to drive Brigadier General Lyon's army from the region, and the realization that the supply situation had not improved "made us feel melancholy," Private Ware wrote.[14] Even worse, rations—never plentiful since the army arrived near Springfield two weeks before—were becoming increasingly scarce for the thousands of Federals under Lyon's command. An Iowa volunteer described a typical member of his regiment this way:

> His beard and hair are long, shaggy, and untrimmed. His hat is pierced with a dozen or more holes of different sizes and shapes in the crown and sides; it has no band, is fringed roughly around the edge of the brim, and comes down over his ears. His flannel shirt is out at the elbows and torn across the back. His pants have lost half of their side stripe, are out at the knees, torn and fringed around the ankles [sic]—and (may I say it to ears polite?) he wears an apron behind that he may not actually touch the ground when he sits down. He has no socks, and his feet peep through his shoes in a half dozen different places, and are only retained upon his feet by a most ingenious application of strings and strips of leather. Until within a day or two past we have been living upon what is called one quarter rations, which means from one-quarter to one-half of a hard cracker at a meal, with coffee once or twice a day, and occasionally a bit of fat bacon or fresh beef as large as one's two fingers.[15]

Ironically, at the same time, readers in Saint Louis were being told by one newspaper that Lyon's army was "now well provisioned, and provided with abundant ammunition," and was being "rapidly increased." It predicted that in a few days an army of twelve to fifteen thousand men would be ready for offensive operations in southwest Missouri.[16] If any of Brigadier General Lyon's volunteers and regulars saw that particular issue of the *Weekly Missouri Democrat*, they probably cursed its editor as they munched their meager rations, mended their tattered uniforms, and prayed for reinforcements, while their beleaguered commander formulated a plan to deal with his (and their) myriad problems.

8

THE SOUTHERN VALLEY FORGE

After their victory at Carthage, Gov. Claiborne Fox Jackson and his State Guardsmen continued to move toward McDonald County in Missouri's extreme southwestern edge, and specifically toward the area known as Cowskin Prairie, where Maj. Gen. Sterling Price had established his camp. On July 6, the State Guardsmen met Confederate Brig. Gen. Ben McCulloch and his force, which had crossed the Missouri line and captured Col. Franz Sigel's lone company at Neosho.

The Missourians were impressed with McCulloch's Confederates. "No wonder that we burst into loud huzzas when the redoubtable McCulloch came into sight, surrounded by his gaily-dressed staff," said Governor Jackson's aide Thomas Snead. The Missourians "looked with delighted eyes on the first Confederate soldiers that we had ever seen. . . . To look like these gallant soldiers; to be of them; to fight beside them for their homes and for our own, was the one desire of all the Missourians."[1] The Texas general was far less impressed with his potential Missouri allies. Snead believed that McCulloch "saw in the Missourians nothing but a half-armed mob, led by an ignorant old militia general."[2] Their union would be a brief one. With the Missouri State Guard now temporarily safe from the Federals, McCulloch, knowing that he had advanced into Missouri without explicit authorization from the Confederate War Department (although he was told that he could cross the border "when necessity and propriety unite," and his superiors later approved of his actions), returned to his camp across the Arkansas border. The State Guard continued on to Cowskin Prairie.

With his troops safely delivered into the hands of Major General Price and his subordinates, Jackson now ended his career as a military commander and returned to his role as civilian leader of the state government. On July 12, he left the state on an incredible odyssey to enlist Confederate help. Putting his considerable political skills to use, Governor Jackson first rode to Little Rock, where he met with Arkansas governor Henry Rector. Jackson went from there to Memphis, Tennessee, for a conference with Gen. Leonidas Polk, and finally, by the end of the month, he had traveled all the way to the Confederate capital in Richmond, Virginia, for an audience with President Jefferson Davis. Although he would not return to southwest Missouri for several weeks, Jackson knew that his troops were in capable hands and that it was far more important for him to recruit help for his cause.

While Jackson did what he could to help the Missourians on the diplomatic front, Price and his generals labored mightily to transform their citizens into soldiers. "I remember few incidents [of Cowskin Prairie]," wrote Lt. William Barlow, "outside of our incessant hard work."[3] Joseph A. Mudd likewise recalled that "the two week's stay here was not a period of repose."[4] Veterans of the Mexican War, the Regular Army, or prewar militia organizations served as drill instructors, moving the green soldiers on the drill field several times a day. John Haskins, a "soldier of fortune" and veteran of William Walker's "filibustering" expedition into Central America a few years before, was a natural drillmaster. One Guardsman recalled: "He humped his shoulders and bent forward, and like a steam tug through a chop sea ploughed the tall prairie grass, his mouth half open and his white incisors gleaming under his shoe-brush mustache" as he demonstrated how to maneuver on a battlefield. Although he was a "most profuse and redundant swearer," his men recognized Haskins as a true leader; it was said that the only thing he enjoyed more than drilling was fighting. When not training, the men made small-arms and artillery cartridges for the upcoming battle with the Federals.

Lt. Col. William Elisha Arnold (pictured with his wife), a graduate of the Virginia Military Institute, fought at Wilson's Creek as the inspector general of the Eighth Division, Missouri State Guard.

The State Guardsmen at Cowskin Prairie were more reminiscent of militia forces of earlier American wars than the armies of the Civil War. Most of the Missourians made do without extensive camp equipage, uniforms, military weapons, or even a variety of rations. Although some were lucky enough to sleep under canvas, many simply bivouacked in the open with their blankets. Civilian clothing was prominent in the ranks, together with civilian shotguns and hunting rifles. Simple rations of beef and flour were issued to new soldiers who tried their hand at cooking in company messes. In some cases, culinary inexperience became painfully obvious. One private, said to be the best cook in his company, was perplexed by a short-age of salt when cooking the beef ration. He simply substituted gunpowder, with disastrous results, forcing his comrades to enjoy only bread that meal. Fortunately, Guardsmen lucky enough to have spending money could purchase foodstuffs from local farmers. Those without could ask for donations from sympathetic civilians.

As Price trained the victors of Carthage, Brigadier General McCulloch camped just across the Arkansas line, likewise drilling and organizing his forces. Unlike his Missouri counter-part, McCulloch carried a commission from the Confederate government in Richmond, with specific orders to defend the Indian Territory (present-day Oklahoma). The Texan led not one state's force but, in effect, a coalition army. In addition to his own Confederate troops (regiments from Louisiana and Arkansas, and eventually one from Texas—a total of about 2,700 men), McCulloch had also been given nominal command of the Arkansas State forces—2,200 state militia troops led by Arkansas brigadier general Nicholas B. Pearce. McCulloch concentrated his mixed force at Camp Walker, near Maysville, Benton County, Arkansas, and nearby Camp Jackson (although later Camp Jackson was abandoned, and the troops there moved to a camp near Bentonville, Arkansas). Like Major General Price, McCulloch forged his troops into an effective combat force during those sweltering July days in northwest Arkansas. "The men are all healthy and in good spirits. They are a fine body of men, and through constant drilling are becoming very efficient. I place a great deal of reliance upon them," he wrote to the Confederate secretary of war.[5] The men also enjoyed visits by ladies from the surrounding country, and a brass band attached to one of the Arkansas regiments furnished "most excellent music" that was "a source of great gratification."[6]

Although McCulloch believed that the Missourians were not prepared for active service, the aggressive Texan pledged to march to Price's aid as he had done earlier when he

NICHOLAS BARTLETT PEARCE

Born in Kentucky in 1828, Pearce graduated from the US Military Academy in 1850, twenty-sixth in his class of forty-four and commissioned a brevet second lieutenant of infantry. Pearce served at various frontier posts in Kansas, Arkansas, and the Indian Territory. He escorted Capt. Randolph Barnes Marcy's expedition to locate Indian reservations in northwestern Texas in 1854 and participated in the Utah Expedition in 1858; although, in his words, he did not take part in any "noted battles," he did participate in scouting against American Indians and took some prisoners. In 1851 Pearce was promoted to second lieutenant and to first lieutenant in 1855; he resigned his commission in 1858 and became a merchant, farmer, and flour manufacturer in Arkansas. Although he opposed his state's secession, he believed it was his duty to stand by his state and his people when Arkansas left the Union; he was named a state brigadier general and appointed to command the First or Western Division of the Army of Arkansas (State Troops). He led that division at the Battle of Wilson's Creek. Following the battle, Pearce's troops returned to their homes, and he was commissioned a major in the Confederate Army and assigned to duty with the subsistence department. He served in the Trans-Mississippi Theater for the remainder of the war but did not see service in the field again. Following the war, Pearce returned to business and died on March 8, 1894, in Dallas, Texas.

captured Neosho; McCulloch believed he could unite his forces with those of Price and actually go on the offensive against Brig. Gen. Nathaniel Lyon. On July 9, McCulloch wrote the Confederate secretary of war: "I think there will be an urgent necessity in the course of a few days to make an attack upon that place [Springfield], or we will receive an attack from their concentrated forces. Should I receive no instructions in the meantime, I think that I will, together with Generals Pearce and Price, make an advance upon it as soon as the different forces are sufficiently organized to take the field."[7] On July 18,

McCulloch confidently stated: "I am anxious to march against them, and if all of the available force now near me could be depended upon I think we could meet with success, or at least cut them off entirely from their supplies and re-enforcements."

But McCulloch also believed that Price's Missourians were badly organized, poorly armed, and almost entirely out of ammunition. Until a "competent military man [was] put in command of the entire force," and until they were better prepared, McCulloch wrote, the Missourians would not advance. "Were these forces properly armed, and supplied with the necessary ammunition," he continued, "I think by rapid concentration we could drive the Federal forces out of Springfield, release the secession prisoners now there, and give our friends a chance of rallying around us. At present, however, the condition of the Missouri forces will not warrant me in marching with my small command. I have therefore chosen a strong position here, and will probably wait until the Missourians are prepared to act. I am satisfied that I can keep back any force that may be sent in this direction."[8]

Despite his misgivings, McCulloch did not wait long to begin his campaign. After giving the Missourians as much ammunition as he could spare, and a precious three weeks in which to organize, McCulloch decided it was time to unite. With Brigadier General Lyon in Springfield, the area around Cowskin Prairie too poor to sustain Price's men indefinitely, and supplies becoming scarce, McCulloch believed that Price would soon be forced to move or disband his forces. By late July, the fiery Texan was ready to march his combined Confederate–Arkansas State force across the line into Missouri to join Price and drive the Federals from Springfield.

9
THE ARMIES COLLIDE

On July 25, Maj. Gen. Sterling Price began moving his troops from Cowskin Prairie to Cassville, the designated rendezvous with the forces of brigadier generals Ben McCulloch and Nicholas Pearce. McCulloch himself arrived three days later. On July 29, McCulloch's men reached Cassville and were greeted with "the wildest enthusiasm" by the Missourians. Amid cheers, the thunder of artillery, and the waving of banners, the Third Louisiana in particular evoked "numerous remarks of praise and admiration" for their marching and discipline.[1]

With the three generals now united and their "coalition" army tentatively formed, the question of an overall commander soon came to the forefront. Price and Pearce naturally turned to the officer who held a commission from Richmond: McCulloch. For the purposes of the campaign in southwest Missouri, McCulloch would lead the "Western Army." In a July 30 message to the Confederate secretary of war, McCulloch vowed to "move towards Springfield as rapidly as possible with the entire force, and hope soon to put the Missourians again in possession of it."[2] He organized the army into three divisions, interspersing his Confederates and Arkansas State troops among the Missouri State Guard units.

Although on the surface all seemed well with the commanders of the Southern coalition army, there existed an underlying current of mistrust fostered by their different backgrounds and experiences. Price and McCulloch had been volunteer officers in the Mexican War, but Price had seen relatively little combat and had pursued a political career after the conflict. To his credit, Price was brave and could inspire the citizen-soldiers of his newly formed State Guard as no other officer could, being driven by his devotion to the cause of Missouri and his desire to "reclaim" the state from the Federals. But as a man with a large ego, Major General Price was known throughout the war for difficulties with superiors (both civilian and military) and fellow generals. His counterpart was equally brave, self-confident, and idolized by his troops, but McCulloch was an unpretentious, practical commander. He had seen considerable action in Mexico, was a student of military history, and was more of an organizer and disciplinarian. McCulloch answered to Jefferson Davis alone and was determined to follow his orders to defend the Indian Territory—and now, with the unstable situation in Missouri, northwest Arkansas. Much like Brig. Gen. Nathaniel Lyon, however, McCulloch was under considerable pressure to achieve decisive results in southwest Missouri.

Rather early in their relationship, one incident in particular underscored the difficult nature of coalition warfare for McCulloch and Price. Even though the Missouri general had agreed to leave his large number of civilian camp followers and unarmed soldiers at Cowskin Prairie, these noncombatants had marched to Cassville. Again McCulloch called on Price to leave them behind. Price agreed, but when the march began again, McCulloch discovered that one of Price's generals had allowed the unarmed men to march with the army. Once more the Texan called on Price's subordinate to leave them behind, but they continued to follow the army anyhow. Even with this burden, on July 31 the Western Army began moving northeast up the Telegraph Road on a fifty-mile march toward Springfield and Lyon.

In Springfield, Lyon and Maj. John M. Schofield, his chief of staff, had spent the last half of July desperately pleading for more supplies and more soldiers to deal with the growing threat to the southwest. Schofield outlined the situation in a letter to Saint Louis: "Our troops are badly clothed, poorly fed, and imperfectly supplied with tents. None of them have as yet been paid, and the three-months' volunteers have become disheartened to such extent that very few of them are willing to renew their enlistment." At least half the Federal army in Springfield was due to be discharged by the middle of August. To make matters worse, an order arrived instructing Lyon to send two of his companies of regulars to Washington, along with Capt. Thomas Sweeny. "Everything seems to combine against me at this point," Lyon believed. Schofield was even blunter. Without reinforcements, he said, "the next news will be of our defeat."[3]

The men in the Federal ranks continued to grumble about the poor conditions. A letter from an Iowan known only as "Mac" noted that the only rations the men received were fresh meat occasionally and cornmeal for mush constantly. "The boys are getting sick, weak and debilitated," he wrote. "Their clothes are ragged and dilapidated, and their shoes cannot be called so any more; they are sandals without soles. We are unfit for duty."[4] To make matters worse, cases of plundering and destruction of property by Federal troops were on the rise, forcing Lyon to issue a general order deploring the "disgraceful" conduct of some of his troops—acts "in violation of his own orders, and contrary to the purpose of the general government." To underscore his displeasure, Lyon assembled his men and had them empty their pockets and knapsacks and pile stolen goods on the ground, with Springfield's merchants then reclaiming their wares. Although these offenders were probably lightly punished, some of Col. Franz Sigel's men who had stolen horses from local farmers were condemned to straddle a painful wooden punishment "horse" for hours in the hot July sun, "exposed to the derision of their comrades and the unsympathetic gaze of the civilians."[5]

Lyon hoped that the July 25 arrival of the new commander of the Western Department, Maj. Gen. John C. Fremont, would start a flow of supplies and reinforcements into southwest Missouri. But even personal messengers sent to Saint Louis by Lyon failed to sway the department commander. Fremont had many pressing concerns in his new command. Although his attention was primarily focused on defending Cairo, the strategic junction of the Mississippi and Ohio Rivers, he was also charged with holding the towns along the Missouri River and dealing with State Guardsmen in the northeast corner of the state.

To the department commander's way of thinking, Lyon could always abandon Springfield, retreat to the railhead at Rolla, and then later move back into southwest Missouri with adequate supplies and reinforcements. Cairo, on the other hand, could not be abandoned, and its loss would be catastrophic. Southeast Missouri, rather than southwest, demanded Fremont's attention. In his opinion, Lyon's decision to stay in Springfield or retreat would be his alone—any disaster that befell him would be Lyon's responsibility. Fremont's lack of support made Lyon even more despondent, but he would not give up trying to convince his superior of the critical situation in southwest Missouri.

Supported or not, the aggressive Brigadier General Lyon was ready to strike another blow by late July. He had received false reports that Brigadier General McCulloch and Major General Price had not united, and not one but three enemy

JOHN C. FREMONT

Born in Georgia in 1813 and appointed a second lieutenant in the US Topographical Engineers in 1838, Fremont led a number of explorations of the West. The first in 1842 took him to Saint Vrain's Fort, Colorado; Fort Laramie, Wyoming; and through South Pass to the Wind River Mountains. Fremont's second expedition in 1843–1844 left Saint Louis, then traveled to the Great Salt Lake and on to Fort Vancouver, then south to Sutter's Fort, to Las Vegas and into northwest Colorado. In his third expedition in 1845, Fremont traveled over the central Rockies to California. He was promoted brevet captain in 1844 and then promoted to lieutenant colonel of the Mounted Rifle Regiment in 1846. Fremont played an important and controversial role in the complex events associated with the seizure of California from Mexico in 1846. He built a crude fort in defiance of Mexican authorities outside Monterey; he assisted the "Bear Flaggers," a group of disgruntled Californios and US settlers who established the "Bear Flag Republic" in Sonoma and declared their independence from Mexico. Upon the arrival of the US Navy in California, Fremont organized the California Battalion, captured San Jose, and assisted in the capture of San Diego and Los Angeles. When Fremont repeatedly refused to obey the orders of California commander Brig. Gen. Stephen W. Kearny, he was arrested and court-

martialed. Convicted of the charge of mutiny, Fremont's sentence was commuted by President James K. Polk, but Fremont resigned from the army anyway in 1848. He served as senator from California, 1850–1851, and became the first presidential candidate of the Republican Party in 1856. Fremont was appointed major general in the US Regular Army in May 1861 and assigned to the command of the Western Department in July 1861. He was relieved of command of the Western Department in November 1861, following the Union defeats at Wilson's Creek and Lexington; his slow pursuit of Missouri State Guard major general Sterling Price; and his controversial emancipation proclamation freeing the slaves of Missourians in rebellion against the United States. Fremont assumed command of the Mountain Department in March 1862; when the Mountain Department was abolished in June 1862, Fremont was assigned command of the First Corps, Army of Virginia, but refused to serve under army commander Gen. John Pope. Fremont was relieved of command at his own request and resigned from the army in 1864. He served as governor of the Arizona Territory from 1878 to 1881. Fremont died on July 13, 1890, in New York City.

columns were on the march from the southwest. Hoping, like Napoleon Bonaparte, to strike each column in turn before they combined, and to keep his men in the ranks with the prospect of seeing action, Lyon led his army out of Springfield on August 1. After spending the first night along Wilson's Creek, his men advanced on the Wire Road in blistering heat and thick dust. "The first day we marched 15 miles, under the hottest sun that ever shone," wrote Charles Clark, a member of the First Iowa. "A soldier in our Regt. that served in India under Gen. [Henry] Havelock," he continued, "says he never suffered more from heat there."[6] Iowa reporter Franc Wilkie guessed the temperature was "anywhere between 1,100 and 2,000 'in the shade,'" and men dropped by the side of the road "as if smitten by lightning."[7] Water and shade were scarce, and the sun was "like a ball of fire," wrote one correspondent, "scorching all animated nature in his way."[8] The Federals were blindly probing for the enemy, moving cautiously and slowly. "We were hunting for McCulloch," wrote Iowan Pvt. Eugene F. Ware, "and did not exactly know where he was."[9] On August 2, the Federals reached Dug Springs, a welcome source of water for the parched troops.

Just to the southwest, McCulloch and Price's men had made camp along Crane Creek. On the morning of August 2, Southern pickets encountered Lyon's advance force—four companies of US regular infantry and Capt. James Totten's Battery. The Southerners quickly fell back before Federal artillery fire and rejoined an advance guard of about 120 Arkansans and Missourians under Capt. Americus V. Rieff.[10] Rieff deployed his men on one side of the road and began skirmishing with the Federals. "Soon we heard the song of our first Minnie balls," Rieff recalled. "It would have been quite interesting, viewed from a safe place, to have seen the boys dodge and their faces blanch. This soon passed off and they were eager to become engaged." Rieff wisely sent a courier to McCulloch, telling him they had encountered Lyon's entire force.

To the south, State Guard Gen. James S. Rains was eating breakfast with his 400-man advance guard. He heard the Federal artillery fire as well and also sent a message to McCulloch asking for assistance. Rains nervously finished his meal and waited for reinforcements to arrive. Finally, early that afternoon, Col. James McIntosh, McCulloch's adjutant, took 150 men and moved up the road to meet Rains. McIntosh reconnoitered the Union position and ordered the Missourian not to bring on a battle but only to test the strength and position of the enemy. If attacked, McIntosh promised Rains support, and then McIntosh returned to camp. Lyon's regulars,

JAMES SPENCER RAINS

Born in Tennessee in 1817, Rains moved to Sarcoxie, Missouri, in 1840. He served as a general in the state militia and was a Newton County judge from 1840 until 1842. Rains won election to the state house in 1844 and later served in the state senate from 1854 through 1861. During this time, he also served as an agent for Indian affairs in various locations, venturing as far as California, where he served as a general in that state's militia. When elected to US Congress in 1861, Rains refused the seat because of his strong Confederate ties.

In 1861, Gov. Claiborne Fox Jackson appointed Rains brigadier general of the Eighth Division, Missouri State Guard. Rains played an active part in the battles of Carthage, Wilson's Creek, Lexington, and Pea Ridge. Without a Confederate commission, he assumed command of mixed Guard and Confederate troops in northwest Arkansas during the fall of 1862. Shortly afterward, General T. C. Hindman relieved Rains of that command for his incompetence and drunkeness.

Afterward Rains moved to Texas to recover his health. He returned to Missouri in 1864 to serve as a military recruiter. After the war, he again returned to Texas where he lived as a farmer, railroad promoter, lawyer, political organizer, and candidate. In 1878, he lost the Texas race for lieutenant governor and died in May 1880. Rains is buried at Lee Cemetery in Dallas County.

deployed as skirmishers, also were ordered not to bring on a battle but to hold until pressed and then fall back on the main Federal force.

About 5:00 p.m., Rains—perhaps stung by West Point graduate McIntosh's dismissive tone, or perhaps in reaction to moves by the Federal skirmishers—began advancing his troops to Dug Springs. By late afternoon, the heat was unbearable and the air "as stifling as a furnace blast" as Rains pushed his men toward the hot, muddy water.

When General Rains and his men came under fire from the nearby Federals, some of his Missourians fled, but the majority deployed on the opposite side of the road from Captain Rieff and his cavalry force. Brigadier General Lyon's regulars stood firm, so Rains sent an aide across the road to Rieff, asking him to coordinate an assault on the Federals. Rieff moved forward, and the Federals began to withdraw. Just then a portion of Company C, First US Cavalry, launched a brave but reckless saber charge, a move that even Rieff admitted was "the most gallant act I saw during the war." They crashed through Rieff's command, cutting and slashing, some halting to engage in hand-to-hand combat. They passed to the rear, toward Rieff's horses, with the owners following them on the run. The Union cavalrymen cut off Rieff and a small group of his men. Then the "business" commenced. When a Union sergeant demanded that they surrender, the Southerners riddled him with buckshot at close range. "We had to move around lively to keep from being tramped [sic] to death," Rieff wrote, but by firing shotguns and pistols at close quarters, they soon unhorsed all their attackers and regained their mounts. On the opposite side of the road, Rains and his State Guardsmen blazed away at the Federals, apparently doing little damage.

What happened next is unclear, although it appears that the regular Federal infantry companies began to fall back in front of Rains, so the State Guardsmen pursued. One correspondent believed Lyon intentionally ordered his men to retire in a move to draw the enemy forward. When Federal artillery (Totten's Battery) opened up again, both the State Guard and Rieff's troopers finally broke and fled in confusion.

Colonel McIntosh, who had not yet made it back to Crane Creek, declined to assist General Rains but did rally most of the fugitives. Although exact losses will never be known, Captain Rieff reported "one man partially scalped with a saber, one dead from exhaustion, one missing, never heard from, and a few slightly wounded."[11] State Guard casualties were probably equally light, and the Federals suffered four killed and seven wounded, all but one cavalrymen from the impetuous saber charge.

"Rains's Scare," as the "affair" at Dug Springs came to be called, dealt another devastating blow to the Price-McCulloch relationship. McCulloch was shocked by what he saw as the "total inefficiency" of Rains's Missourians, who, he inaccurately reported, "were put to flight by a single cannon-shot, running in the greatest confusion, without the loss of a single man except

one, who died of overheat or sun-stroke, and bringing no reliable information as to the position or force of the enemy."[12] The Texan had never been completely comfortable trusting his new allies; now, in their first test of arms under a unified command, he believed the State Guard had failed miserably.[13]

Even though he had won the day at Dug Springs and tested the mettle of part of McCulloch's army, Brigadier General Lyon was still troubled. One regular saw him sitting in the doorway of a nearby cabin after the fighting, twirling the stem of a flower between his fingers, looking "full of anxiety and trouble."[14] The day after the skirmish, Lyon pushed his army a few

JAMES McQUEEN McINTOSH

Born in Florida in 1828, McIntosh graduated from the US Military Academy in 1849, last in his class of forty-three. He was promoted to brevet second lieutenant of infantry in 1849 and served at various posts in Texas until 1855. He took part in the Sioux Expedition of 1855 and peacekeeping duty in Kansas in 1856. McIntosh was advanced to second lieutenant in 1851, first lieutenant (First Cavalry) in 1855, and captain in 1857; he saw action against the Cheyenne at the Battle of Solomon's Fork in 1857 and skirmishes with the Kiowas and Comanches in 1860. He was stationed at Fort Smith, Arkansas, when the Civil War began; McIntosh resigned his commission in May 1861 and joined the Confederate service. He served as colonel of the Second Arkansas Mounted Rifles and as Brig. Gen. Benjamin McCulloch's adjutant during the Wilson's Creek Campaign. Promoted to brigadier general in January 1862, McIntosh led a cavalry brigade at the Battle of Pea Ridge, Arkansas, and was killed there on March 7, 1862.

miles farther south to the little settlement of Curran, a wide spot in the road with one building that functioned as a post office, general store, and tavern. Although the Federals formed a line of battle after they spied several hundred mounted Southerners, the enemy soon vanished, adding to the Federal belief that they were being drawn closer to McCulloch's position. Skirmishing erupted as Lyon's troops again moved cautiously forward. They halted for the night at a place called McCullah's Store.

On the morning of August 4, for the first time in the campaign, the normally decisive Lyon held a council of war to chart his next course of action. Lyon told the fifteen or so officers present that it appeared the enemy would not risk a battle until they were united, but he believed their columns were now in supporting distance of one another. Spies had told him that about fifteen thousand enemy troops now were only about six miles away. Lyon told his officers the size of the Federal army, that he expected no reinforcements, and that they would soon be reduced to salt and fresh beef, with many men sick and some barefoot. Worse, Brigadier General McCulloch's cavalry could move behind them, cut them off from Springfield, and even capture the city. A decisive battle had not yet occurred, and even if the army pushed forward to a victory, it could not capitalize on the win and might be lost. On the other hand, if the Federals retreated to Springfield and made a stand there, the enemy would divide their forces to attack the city and might be defeated in detail. Lyon then asked if the army should pursue the Southerners further, fall back to Springfield, and wait for reinforcements and supplies, or fall back to Springfield and act according to circumstances. Except for Colonel Sigel, who voted to attack, it appears that every other officer voted for a retreat. Just at that moment, when the officers were ready to decide how far to retreat, word came that the Federal pickets were under attack, and the council of war broke up. For now, the army would fall back at least as far as Springfield.[15]

The march back was just as disagreeable as the march out had been. The stifling heat, lack of water, fatigue, and anxiety about a possible attack on the retreating column added to the Union soldiers' belief that the whole expedition had been a failure. Lyon's men staggered back into Springfield on the morning of August 5. Lyon's officers then considered whether the army should remain at Springfield, build defenses, and wait until reinforcements arrived, or continue to retreat to Rolla or Fort Scott, Kansas. Lyon consulted several officers, including his closest subordinates. Some wanted to fall back to Fort Scott, others to Rolla, while some, like Sigel, wanted to go to Rolla or retreat only until they met with reinforcements. A great many citizens urged Lyon to remain. As options were discussed, the troops remained under arms. Finally, after three or four hours of deliberation, Lyon ordered his men into camp—they would stay in Springfield. His officers agreed. Captain Sweeny

believed that "Lyon came very near abandoning this place," but "better counsels prevailed," and the Federals were now determined to hold on as long as possible, for "if we give up this place all will be lost."[16]

Supplies were scarce. Charles Clark of the First Iowa complained, "It is almost impossible to get sufficient provisions here for the command. For the last two weeks we have had nothing but flour and beef." He said, "We manage to get a few ears of green corn, now and then, and the race of chickens has long since become extinct, in this benighted region." Even though the situation was bleak and "Fears are entertained by some that we may be surrounded . . . and our retreat cut off," Clark, at least, was sure that his comrades would make the enemy pay: "If that should transpire our boys feel mad enough to make an awful fight of it."[17]

As Lyon's men began to retreat back to Springfield, Brigadier General McCulloch faced some difficult decisions of his own. With the lackluster performance of the Missourians at Dug Springs, it is possible that McCulloch decided to remain in his defensive position at Crane Creek and wait for Lyon's advance. The Texan called together Brigadier General Pearce, Major General Price, and the other Missouri generals and posed "the question of the advance." Accounts differ about what happened next. According to Thomas L. Snead, Price's aide,[18] McCulloch contemplated retreat, so Price threatened to break the fragile coalition army apart and move forward on his own if McCulloch did not issue orders to advance. According to Pearce, on the other hand, McCulloch did not mention retreat but was reluctant to advance without explicit orders from Richmond. Whatever McCulloch contemplated, Price, Pearce, and the others were "anxious and impatient" to move forward. Apparently, no consensus was reached, so another council of war was held the next day. This time, Pearce recalled, McCulloch announced that he had received the necessary orders from the Confederate capital, and the army would move.

As McCulloch had already been given permission by the Confederate War Department to advance into Missouri, it seems unlikely that Pearce's version of events is entirely correct, but it is more reliable than Snead's partisan account. Undoubtedly, McCulloch and his closest subordinates had serious doubts about the reliability of their Missouri allies; McCulloch might have been using the lack of orders from Richmond as an excuse to buy more time to consider his options and formulate a plan. Perhaps he was merely waiting to see what Lyon's next move would be. It is highly doubtful that he was thinking seriously about retreating. Whatever the reason for the delay, McCulloch's decision to march was no doubt influenced by the fact that he received word, not from Richmond, as Pearce remembered, but from Gen. Leonidas Polk, who sent the welcome news that Confederate troops were advancing into southeast Missouri and could cooperate with his force.

It is likely that Price and McCulloch had some sort of heated confrontation during this period, either at the council of war or perhaps privately. This confrontation eventually resulted in compromise. Although Price had already informally agreed to serve under McCulloch's command several days before, he may in fact have threatened to dissolve the coalition if the army did not advance. In return for McCulloch ordering his men to move up the Wire Road after the Federals, Price made the command arrangement more formal. On August 4, he officially announced to his men that McCulloch was now the "supreme commander" of the coalition forces, and the Missourians were directly subject to his orders.

The same day, Brigadier General McCulloch issued explicit orders to the men of his Western Army. The troops would march at midnight to meet the Federals. Shouting and drum-beating were prohibited, and the "strictest silence" was to be observed. The men were ordered to take full canteens and one day's cooked rations. A sufficient amount of ammunition was to be distributed, and no unarmed men would march. No wagons would follow—the men would move quickly and be in position to strike the Federals the next morning. Finally, McCulloch reminded his men that the eyes of their eastern comrades who had won the victory at Bull Run would be upon them. He urged his western soldiers to give their comrades a second victory.[19]

The Southerners spent the afternoon and evening of August 4 preparing for a decisive battle. Some cooked their meager rations of flour and meat, others distributed ammunition, and still others wrote what they believed might be their final letters home. "We were nervous, restless, sleepless," wrote Texan Samuel B. Barron.[20] By midnight, as ordered, the Southerners were on the march. "The silence and steadiness of that march in the dark night up that solitary road, lined on each side with the black frowning woods, seemed truly grand," wrote William Watson.[21] Fellow Louisianan W. H. Tunnard likewise noted that his comrades marched "in breathless silence" and "in anticipation of meeting almost certain death, but with undaunted, unquailing spirits."[22]

But while the spirit was willing in the Southern ranks, occasionally the flesh was found wanting. Thomas Bacon, a Missouri State Guardsman, observed that his comrades noiselessly moved out onto the main road, only to flinch when some unidentified soldier nervously discharged his fowling piece. Bacon soon fell sound asleep while marching and fell out of the ranks, only to be startled awake, return to his proper place, and repeat the experience.[23] Morning came, and the Southerners soon found the abandoned Federal camp; at least some officers presumed that either Brigadier General Lyon had overestimated the enemy's strength or else he was drawing them farther away from their supplies and into a trap.

Now the race was on, with the Southerners forced to suffer along the Wire Road the same as their foes. McCulloch ordered the advance to continue—cautiously at first, for fear of stumbling into a Federal ambush. Watson noted that the road had not been obstructed or crops destroyed, further supporting the notion that Lyon was "inviting" them into a trap. The frustrated McCulloch took a small group of well-armed Texans and galloped ahead to personally reconnoiter the Federal army, inspiring the men in the ranks to push rapidly ahead.

"All that day we raced along," wrote Bacon. "The dust was thick and gritty. It was a fearful march. I remember one [water] well . . . but the soldiers soon exhausted it. Masses of them swarmed and crowded around that well . . . and I moved on in despair." Despite the best efforts of Bacon and his thirsty comrades, plowing through heat and dust, they were not able to catch up with the fleeing Federals and bring them to battle. Bacon panted through the dust, the narrow stock of his hunting rifle feeling as though it was "severing my collar bone." "The march . . . was, perhaps, the hardest ever made by any army," wrote Joseph A. Mudd, with the heavy growth along the road "shutting off the slightest motion of air." Men were so thickly coated by dust as to be almost unrecognizable, and their thirst "almost maddening." Desperate for water, Mudd drank from a stagnant pool covered with thick, green scum.[24]

Capt. Reuben Kay, a graduate of the Kentucky Military Institute, was a volunteer aid to Col. John Taylor Hughes (First Infantry Regiment, Fourth Division, Missouri State Guard) at Wilson's Creek. When the regiment's adjutant was mortally wounded early in the action, Kay assumed his duties.

The Southerners finally arrived at Moody's Spring, only to find the watering hole crowded with men. Bacon and his friends fell into line to get water, but by nightfall they still had not quenched their thirst. Despite the protests of their officers, the officer in charge at the spring insisted that units wait their turn, and the State Guardsmen broke ranks with parched throats. "It would not have taken much to start a fratricidal fight for access to the spring," Bacon wrote. The men then camped near a muddy creek, their sole source of drinking water. To make matters worse, that night there was a thunderstorm, and countless horses stampeded. Although the horses did not come their way, it triggered panic in the ranks of Bacon's company.[25]

The following day, McCulloch moved his command about a mile to the valley of Wilson's Creek, an area tailor-made for his army, possessing abundant water, crops, grass, and firewood, and astride the Wire Road, the major highway to Springfield. McCulloch deployed his men for two miles along the creek. At the southern end of the valley, on the flat plateau that formed the farm of Joseph Sharp, a mixed force of cavalrymen was camped, including McCulloch's South Kansas–Texas Cavalry and the First Arkansas Mounted Rifles, Pearce's First Arkansas Cavalry, and two Missouri State Guard cavalry units, led by Col. Benjamin Brown and Lt. Col. James Major—in all, about 2,450 soldiers. Just north of the Sharp farm, between Wilson's Creek and the base of a commanding height later to be called "Bloody Hill," Price gathered 1,600 infantrymen around his headquarters at the cabin of William B. Edwards. These men represented the State Guard's Third, Fourth, Sixth, and Seventh Divisions, commanded by Gens. John B. Clark, William Y. Slack, M. M. Parsons, and James McBride, respectively, and Capt. Henry Guibor's State Guard Battery. On Bloody Hill itself were the 284 men of Col. Benjamin Rives's cavalry of General Slack's division. At the northern end of the encampment, near the mill and house of John Gibson, was a large brigade of Missouri State Guard cavalrymen (about 1,200 troopers) under the command of Col. James Cawthorn.

Camped on the eastern side of Wilson's Creek was about half the army, including the rest of Brigadier General Pearce's brigade (Charles Carroll's Cavalry Company, the Third, Fourth, and Fifth Arkansas Infantry, Capt. John Reid's Fort Smith Battery, and Capt. William Woodruff's Pulaski Battery—a total of nearly 1,900); Col. Richard Weightman's Missouri State Guard infantry brigade (1,300 men); Capt. Hiram Bledsoe's State Guard Battery (strength unknown); and the remainder of McCulloch's command (the Second Arkansas Mounted Rifles, Dandridge McRae's Battalion, and Louis Hébert's Third Louisiana Infantry—about 1,320 troops).

LOUIS HÉBERT

Born in Iberville Parish, Louisiana, in 1820, Hébert was the son of a prosperous sugar plantation owner. After completing his primary education with private tutors, he attended Jefferson College and earned an appointment to the US Military Academy, from which he graduated in 1845, third out of a class of forty-one. In 1846, he resigned his commission to help his ailing father manage the family plantation but resumed his military profession as a major and later colonel in the state militia. In 1853, Hébert was elected to the state senate and was later appointed as Louisiana's chief engineer. He was serving on the Board of Public Works when secession occurred. Hébert was elected colonel of the Third Louisiana Infantry, which quickly garnered a reputation as being one of the best-trained and hardest fighting regiments in the Western Theater. Ordered to Missouri in 1861, Hébert and his Louisianans won praise for their prominent role at Wilson's Creek, after which he was given command of a brigade under Maj. Gen. Sterling Price. While leading an unsuccessful attack at Pea Ridge on March 7, 1862, Hébert was surrounded and captured with a number of his men. After being exchanged, he returned to the army and was promoted to brigadier general on May 26. In September 1862, he led his reorganized brigade into furious fighting at Iuka, assuming command of the division when its commander, Brig. Gen. Henry Little, was killed. Hébert continued to command the division at the Battle of Corinth in October, where he performed effectively on the first day of battle but mysteriously  reported himself ill—for reasons that are still unclear—before the final assault on the second day. After Corinth, he returned to brigade command and served with distinction throughout the Vicksburg Campaign. After the surrender of the garrison in Vicksburg, Hébert was once again exchanged and transferred to North Carolina, where he oversaw the heavy artillery around Fort Fisher and served as chief engineer of the Department of North Carolina until the end of the war. In the postwar years, Hébert returned to his home state of Louisiana, where he edited a newspaper and taught at private schools in Iberville and St. Martin Parishes. He died on January 7, 1901, and was buried in Breaux Bridge, Louisiana. Aside from the second day of Corinth, Hébert had a solid record of tactical leadership throughout the war. Interestingly, he was the first cousin of Confederate brigadier general Paul O. Hébert and a brother-in-law of Confederate brigadier general Walther H. Stevens.

Wilson's Creek at the foot of Bloody Hill, circa 1883.

In and around the scattered farm fields and open prairie land lived about a dozen families (approximately one hundred people). In addition to the families of Gibson, Edwards, and Sharp were the families of E. B. Short and federal postmaster John A. Ray. Much like the rest of Missouri, the civilians in this area were divided. Although we do not know the political sentiments of some of the major landowners (notably John Gibson), we can safely guess that the Sharp family was pro-secessionist, whereas the Edwards, Ray, and Short families supported the Union cause. Whether civilian or soldier, all those permanently or only temporarily living along Wilson's Creek believed that only ten miles farther up the Wire Road lay Lyon, the Federal army, Springfield—and for the Southern army—victory.

10
LYON'S DIFFICULT DECISION

With the Southerners now only ten miles from Springfield, the residents of the city (largely pro-Union in sympathy) began to grow quite anxious about how long it might be before the city changed hands. Rumors were afoot that while Brig. Gen. Ben McCulloch's main army was camped along Wilson's Creek, two other forces were flanking the city. Stores were vacated, and residents began to consider which of their most valuable articles could be easily transported. "All together it was a sad sight to witness," wrote one onlooker. The local bank even offered to loan the government $250,000 with the idea that if the army retreated, the funds would not fall into rebel hands. (The offer was accepted.) When Union scouts reported that the roads near the city were clear, civilian fears eased, although they undoubtedly believed that with two determined armies close by, something dramatic was bound to happen soon.[1]

With his return to Springfield, Brig. Gen. Nathaniel Lyon was forced to deal again with his recurring problem: a lack of men and supplies. His Iowans were due for discharge on August 14. The soldiers of the Fifth Missouri were scheduled to be released at different times, from August 9 to August 18, and most of the Third Missouri soldiers were scheduled for release at the same time. The general would soon be left with only thirty-five hundred men. The prospect of reinforcements continued to be discouraging. On the night of August 5, Capt. John Cavender of the First Missouri Infantry met with Lyon and brought more depressing news. Lyon had sent the Missourian to Maj. Gen. John C. Fremont just after the latter had arrived in Saint Louis. (In fact, Cavender was one of at least six personal messengers sent to Fremont to plead the case of Lyon.) Cavender had a brief meeting with the general to impress upon him the seriousness of Lyon's situation; Cavender had been promised both reinforcements and pay for Lyon's troops. But Cavender did not return with any specifics, so Lyon continued to fear that, with such empty promises, he would remain on his own.

Although some historians have criticized Fremont for abandoning Lyon, in fact he had made some effort (albeit too late) to send additional troops to Springfield. In command of the Western Department less than a week, and fixated on the possible capture of the strategic town of Cairo by the Confederates, the department commander had left Saint Louis for Cairo with thirty-eight hundred reinforcements on August 1. Three days later, with Cairo secured, Fremont returned to Saint Louis. The same day, he ordered Col. James Montgomery's Third Kansas Infantry to march immediately from Fort Leavenworth, Kansas, to join Lyon.[2] Apparently he also ordered Col. John D. Stevenson's Seventh Missouri Infantry to march from Boonville to Rolla, and then on to Springfield, and Fremont later claimed to have ordered Col. John Wyman's Thirteenth Illinois from Rolla to reinforce Lyon as well. If in fact Fremont ordered all three of these regiments to go to Lyon's assistance, none reached the beleaguered general in Springfield. Colonels Stevenson and Wyman never left Rolla because of a lack of transportation, and Colonel Montgomery did not move out of Kansas.

With or without supplies or reinforcements, however, the soldiers in Brigadier General Lyon's army were grimly determined to strike a decisive blow against the enemy in southwest Missouri. An eyewitness reported that the officers and men in Springfield were "eager for a fight"—"as eager for a fight as hungry wolves." Capt. Thomas Sweeny wrote a friend: "We would be satisfied if we could only get the rascals to fight us, but they know better than that, for every time we go out to meet them they run off. We'll catch them yet one of these fine mornings; see if we don't."[3] On the other hand, some Union soldiers probably agreed with Iowan private Eugene F. Ware that with a superior force of the enemy so close to Springfield, they had little choice but to fight. "It looked to us boys that escape was impossible and that we must fight."[4]

The exhausted commander of the Army of the West called a council of war on the night of August 7. Again Lyon argued that the army should stay in Springfield, while most of his officers voted for retreat to Rolla or Fort Scott. According to an account written by Sweeny (who claimed to have missed the meeting), Lyon agreed with his officers' decision to abandon Springfield. Everything was prepared, and the troops waited for the order to move. Sweeny strongly disagreed with this decision and, during a long private conversation with Lyon, used "forcible language" to convince his commander that they should remain in Springfield—long enough to give battle to the enemy. He argued that the Federals would lose more men in a summer retreat of more than one hundred miles than they would in a battle. If they attempted to retreat, they would be encumbered with a slow wagon train and hundreds of civilian refugees, and the unbeaten enemy had a large number of cavalrymen familiar with the country who could harass the column. Even worse, if the Confederate forces in southeast Missouri got wind of the retreat, they would block it and guarantee Lyon's destruction.

Captain Sweeny pointed out that when he had arrived in Springfield, before Lyon, he had promised to protect the many pro-Union civilians in the area. If they abandoned the city without a fight, these supporters would become disgusted and lose confidence in the Union cause, and possibly even go over to the Confederacy. If Missouri fell, he explained, then, just like dominoes, the other border states would "go out." Finally, and perhaps most importantly, to abandon Springfield without a fight risked ruining the reputation of the army's commander and every officer under him. When Lyon asked Sweeny what he would do, the captain told him to wait patiently until the enemy came within easy marching distance, then march out and launch a surprise attack if possible, as the odds always favored the attacker. Lyon expressed fears that the army would be destroyed if they failed, but Sweeny argued that even defeated, the army would be in better shape to retreat than without risking a battle.[5] Lyon, temporarily swayed by Sweeny's arguments, did not issue the orders that would put his troops on the road to Rolla. The army would stay in Springfield for the moment to see how the situation developed, and it would leave only if forced out by the enemy.

After a false report arrived the next day that the Southern army was within two miles of Springfield, Lyon called another council on the night of August 8. That night's question was the one posed the night before by Sweeny: whether to retreat without giving the enemy battle, risking a fight every mile of the retreat, or to strike the Southerners and cripple them so that they could not follow. No doubt convinced by Sweeny and Lyon, all the officers present agreed to move against the Southerners, although they disagreed with Col. Franz Sigel's suggestion to divide the army into two columns (one commanded by Lyon, the other by himself) to strike the enemy from opposite directions.

With that major decision now set in stone, Lyon ordered that the exhausted army would rest for a day and move from

JOSEPH BENNETT PLUMMER

Born in Massachusetts in 1816, Plummer graduated from the US Military Academy in 1841, twenty-second in his class of fifty-two. He was commissioned a second lieutenant in the First Infantry in 1841 and stationed at posts in Wisconsin, Iowa, and Missouri until the start of the Mexican War. Plummer served in the Vera Cruz and Mexico City garrisons during the Mexican War and advanced to first lieutenant in the First Infantry in 1848. He served on the frontier at various posts in Texas and was promoted to captain in 1852. Plummer joined Brig. Gen. Nathaniel Lyon's Army of the West and served as the commander of a battalion of US Regulars during the Wilson's Creek Campaign, where he was severely wounded. In September, he was promoted to colonel of the Eleventh Missouri Infantry; Plummer led Federal forces to victory at the Battle of Fredericktown, Missouri, the following month, routing Missouri State Guard forces in what Gen. Ulysses S. Grant termed "an important victory." In October 1861, Plummer was named a brigadier general of volunteers; in March 1862, he participated in the capture of New Madrid, Missouri. He also participated in the advance on Corinth, Mississippi, and the subsequent siege there from April to May 1862. Near Corinth, on August 9, 1862, Plummer died from the effects of his Wilson's Creek wound.

Springfield the next evening. In the words of Capt. Joseph Plummer, one of Lyon's old classmates from West Point, the Federals would "make a bold dash on them when our men were full of courage and animation, and whip them or cripple them."[6]

The stakes were high for the Army of the West. Lyon had been largely successful since the campaign began in June. He had secured the state capital and the Missouri River and had driven the State Guard into southwest Missouri. But now he faced his greatest challenge. With supplies low and his army physically exhausted and on the verge of dissolution, Lyon would not force his men to undertake a disgraceful retreat without a fight. To prove himself to Major General Fremont and his superiors in Washington, he would gamble that his mixed force of regulars and volunteers could deal the enemy a crippling blow. His troops were eager to test their mettle. The Battle of Wilson's Creek was scheduled for the early morning of August 10, 1861.

11

THE ARMIES PREPARE

Despite the rumors in Springfield of an imminent Southern attack on the town, most of Brig. Gen. Ben McCulloch's Western Army spent August 6–9 in their camps along Wilson's Creek, "rather inactive," in the words of Louisiana soldier William Watson. The Southerners recovered from their trying march from Cassville, built brush arbors and other improvised shelters, cared for their mounts and weapons, and waited for their commanders to decide when they would fight the decisive battle with the Federals in town. Missouri Guardsman Thomas Bacon later recalled how the men feasted on roasted ears of corn and jerked beef, with the apparatus necessary to smoke and dry the beef giving their camp "a woe-begone and barbarous appearance, an unpleasant indication of a relapse from civilization. Crusoe's savages would have made precisely such a showing."[1] Dr. John Snyder of the State Guard likewise recalled a diet of tough corn, tougher beef, and creek water, with coffee and whiskey "unattainable luxuries to all but a favored few."[2]

Wilson's Creek Battleground from a distance, circa 1883.

Ironically, though Brig. Gen. Nathaniel Lyon's troops were low on supplies and were preparing to launch a desperate surprise attack, some Southerners saw themselves as the underdogs in any future encounter. A Louisiana soldier wrote that everyone knew the Federals were entrenching themselves in Springfield, where they were "all right," and now the Southerners would have to "force the fighting." "They were resting upon their base of operations, in a commanding position, with abundance of supplies," wrote Watson, "and their force likely to be augmented." On the other hand, McCulloch's army was low on supplies, far from their base of operations, with a failing transportation system and a great deal of distance, bad roads, creeks, and rivers between them and their base. "We had no chance of reinforcements," he wrote, "and our strength was likely to be decreased by sickness."[3]

Though each Southerner in the coalition army knew that a fight loomed, no one, not even the army's commander, was exactly sure when it would happen. McCulloch relied on Maj.

Gen. Sterling Price and his local State Guardsmen for reports on the strength and position of the enemy, but the commanding general complained that in fact the Missourians supplied no useful information, and the information he did receive was "very conflicting and unsatisfactory." As if to prod the State Guardsmen to reconnoiter Springfield and gauge the strength and condition of Lyon's force, McCulloch threatened to march the army back to Cassville rather than risk an attack on an unknown enemy. McCulloch himself, harkening back to his days as a scout and Texas Ranger in the Mexican War, left camp to scout the Federal position. On these "excursions," as Brig. Gen. Nicholas Pearce termed them, McCulloch would take potshots at the Federal pickets with his rifle, "much to their discomfiture and greatly to his amusement."

McCulloch did no better in his attempts to get information from the local civilian population. Unlike Price, McCulloch was unsure of the reliability of some of his local civilian informants, considering them of questionable loyalty, easily deceived, or prone to exaggeration. A State Guard surgeon saw more sinister motives in the visits by many civilians to the Southern camp, including innocent farmers looking for lost stock, new recruits, peddlers, and even fine ladies visiting friends in the camp. They were, in fact, Union spies, he argued, who seemed sympathetic and wished the Southerners success but were "surprisingly ignorant" of the happenings in Springfield and told "many widely conflicting stories."[4]

But then the Southerners enjoyed a stroke of luck. On August 9, two women in Springfield with a pass through the Federal lines left town in a buggy, evaded outlying Union pickets, and took a "circuitous route" to Major General Price's headquarters, arriving about three o'clock that afternoon. Although Lyon had the roads leading into Springfield strongly picketed, so civilians could enter but not leave, he probably thought the women could be trusted or, if engaged in some spying mission, would be detected by his guards if they attempted to deviate from their route. The women brought important intelligence, including the position and number of the Federal troops and the number of enemy artillery pieces.

McCulloch immediately called a council of war. The officers decided that rather than wait for Lyon to strike, the Southerners would leave Wilson's Creek that night at 9:00 p.m. and move into position to attack Springfield the following morning. Four columns or divisions, under the command of brigadier generals McCulloch and Pearce, Major General Price, Gen. James McBride, and Col. Elkanah Greer, plus a cavalry force under Gen. James S. Rains, would strike the town simultaneously from different directions at daybreak. McCulloch, undoubtedly not entirely convinced of the accuracy of the information brought by the two female civilians, felt he had little choice—it was either "a disastrous retreat or a blind attack upon Springfield. The latter was preferred."[5]

When the long-delayed march order was announced, the tranquil camps became scenes of commotion as the eager Southerners prepared for the final showdown with Lyon. "The scene of preparation . . . was picturesque and animating in the extreme," wrote Pearce, as knots of men gathered to prepare ammunition for the coming fight.[6] "The universal feeling in the command . . . was one of joy," said Pearce, when the long-wished-for order finally arrived. The men were motivated by a desire "to take revenge for having forced them from their homes and firesides and to punish them for their impudence and temerity."[7] Some fitted new flints in the locks of their flintlock muskets; others divided percussion caps and distributed what little ammunition was available. Others drew out molds and began casting bullets and making cartridges. Tents were struck, arms were inspected, and at least some Southerners drew and cooked one day's rations, filled haversacks, packed knapsacks, and loaded cooking utensils.

In Springfield, the Federals spent August 9 preparing as well. Early that morning, Lyon received another message from

ELKANAH BRACKIN GREER

Born in Tennessee in 1825, Greer grew up in Mississippi and served under Col. Jefferson Davis in the First Mississippi Regiment ("Mississippi Rifles") during the Mexican War. After the war, Greer moved to Marshall, Texas, and became a planter and lawyer. Greer, an ardent secessionist and anti-abolitionist, was a leader of the Knights of the Golden Circle; he attended the 1860 Democratic Party convention in Charleston as a delegate and offered the services of a battalion of Texans to the state of South Carolina immediately after Abraham Lincoln's election. Greer was commissioned colonel of the South Kansas–Texas (Third Texas) Cavalry, the first Texas regiment organized for service outside the state, in June 1861. He led that regiment at the battles of Wilson's Creek and Pea Ridge, March 7–8, 1862. Commissioned a brigadier general in October 1862, Greer was appointed "commandant of conscripts" for the Trans-Mississippi Department by Gen. Edmund Kirby Smith. Although referred to as "an officer of energy and capacity," Greer found himself in an unpopular position and made enemies carrying out his duties. General Kirby Smith expressed his deep appreciation of Greer's services, noting that he worked hard and intelligently and despite many difficulties had brought order to the conscription bureau. Despite his success, the Confederate War Department relieved him of his command in March 1865. Greer died in Devall's Bluff, Arkansas, on March 25, 1877.

Maj. Gen. John C. Fremont, dated August 6, which said that if he could not maintain his position, he should fall back to Rolla—reinforcing Lyon's belief that if he stayed in Springfield, he did so of his own responsibility. Lyon's pent-up frustration finally burst out: "God damn General Fremont," he exclaimed, but then calmed himself and wrote what was undoubtedly the last message of his life. "I find my position extremely embarrassing," he admitted. He was still not able to decide whether to hold his position or retire. If surrounded, he wrote, he knew he must retire. "I shall hold my ground as long as possible, though I may . . . endanger the safety of my entire force." He wrote that he fully expected the enemy to attack, but he made no mention of his plan to strike the Southerners the following morning. Perhaps he was still not entirely convinced that an attack could be successful; perhaps he believed that somehow the Army of the West could win a decisive victory and hold Springfield until reinforcements and supplies arrived.

About midmorning, Col. Franz Sigel visited Lyon again to argue for an independent role. After a two-hour meeting, Lyon agreed to the two-pronged attack plan. Historians have since tried to explain why Lyon chose to divide his command in the face of a superior enemy. Some have argued that the general was intimidated by Sigel's popularity. With so much of the army made up of Saint Louis Germans—men who saw Sigel as an inspirational and talented commander—Lyon may have been reluctant to oppose Sigel's plan and lose the support of a large part of his force. Others believe that Lyon was genuinely impressed by Sigel's knowledge of military history and the tactical skill he had demonstrated on battlefields in Europe and the United States. It could be that Lyon fervently believed that such a daring maneuver would ensure the destruction of the enemy. Unfortunately, the evidence is contradictory, and we will probably never know for sure what motivated Lyon in those last few hours of his life.

At 4:00 p.m., Lyon called his last council of war. Despite the objections of his officers, he announced that Sigel's plan would be put into effect. Lyon would take about 4,200 men and strike the northern edge of the enemy encampment. Sigel would take his brigade, about 1,200 men (two infantry regiments, two cavalry companies, and a six-gun artillery battery), and move against the southern end of Brigadier General McCulloch's force. The army would march at 6:00 p.m.

Accompanied by part of his staff, Brigadier General Lyon approached each company of his command and made a brief speech, perhaps only a minute long. Opinions about the effectiveness of this prebattle motivational talk were varied. Some recalled that Lyon spoke in a "quiet, soldierly way," telling them he expected to attack the enemy the following morning and cautioning them to maintain absolute silence. "Thus was seen a Regular Army officer, a trained soldier, noted as a strict disciplinarian, confiding in his volunteers the preliminary movements incident to a battle against immense odds," explained Iowan Andrew Geddes.[8] Pvt. Henry O'Connor of Company A of the First Iowa remembered a more passionate speech from their commander: "Boys, we may have warm work to-morrow. . . . The honor of Iowa and the interests of your country are in your hands, and I want you to maintain them." He noted that the next company in line carried Springfield muskets; he told them how he expected them "to make good use of them tomorrow" and how to resist charges by the enemy's large cavalry force.[9]

Another Iowan, Pvt. Eugene F. Ware, was far less impressed. He wrote that Lyon gave a "tactless and chilling speech," lacking in "dash, vim, or encouragement"—"a very poor effort and entirely wanting in enthusiasm."[10] Another soldier thought he could detect "traces of deep anxiety in his countenance and his voice," the latter "more subdued and milder than usual."[11] About 5:00 p.m., the first Federals began to march from Springfield, and by about 6:30, all the regiments had joined the column under Lyon moving west along the Mount Vernon–Little York Road. About the same time, Colonel Sigel began moving his brigade south from their camp toward Wilson's Creek.

Along Wilson's Creek, the Southerners formed ranks about sunset, commands assumed their positions, and the anxious men waited for 9:00 p.m. and the order to begin marching toward Springfield. Just before the critical hour, clouds began to roll in, distant thunder boomed, and rain began to fall. In practically every other Civil War campaign, a light shower did not deter troops or their officers from carrying out their assigned missions. But Brigadier General McCulloch's force was no ordinary Civil War army. Many men had no leather boxes to protect their paper cartridges and keep their gunpowder dry—perhaps no more than one in four had that important accoutrement. Some carried ammunition in their pockets or in canvas bags or haversacks. Others had shot pouches and powder horns. Some carried flintlock muskets that were even more susceptible to moisture. Few men had bayonets. McCulloch simply could not risk having his men caught in a downpour on the road to Springfield, leaving many with wet powder and percussion caps, unable to fight the next morning. After consulting with Major General Price, McCulloch reluctantly ordered his men to rest on their arms and await further orders. As the major of the Third Louisiana explained to one of his men, "It would never do for us to attempt this job and make a botch of it."[12]

Unfortunately, a "botched job" was already in the making. Cavalry pickets north, south, and east of the camps had been withdrawn in anticipation of the march. With movement orders expected at any time, no one in McCulloch's command thought of sending the pickets back out to their positions. To his credit, however, when McCulloch heard late that night of enemy movement west of Springfield, he ordered a small detachment from his own scout company to a position on the prairie in sight of town at daylight to verify the report's accuracy. These men would, in fact, encounter Brigadier General Lyon's army and return to camp to report, but their warning was too little, too late. McCulloch's blunder with the camp's pickets would guarantee that the Southerners would have virtually no warning of the approach of an enemy force.

Although the suspense of waiting for orders was becoming unbearable to McCulloch's men, those soldiers fortunate enough to have tents pitched them again. Others did their best to find a dry place to sleep out in the open. Missouri State Guardsman Bacon robbed the mules of hay, placed his rifle, ammunition, and caps on the hay, covered them with his felt hat, and lay face down on them and let the rain fall on his back. He did not sleep soundly, as he kept expecting marching orders. "The night wore drearily away," he recalled.

Others were able to get a decent rest, especially after the rain stopped about 11:00 p.m. and no orders were forthcoming. "We had a good night's sleep," recalled State Guardsman John P. Bell, "with no dreams of the to-morrow, for we had no conception of what a tomorrow's battle was like, all our so-called battles having been practically one-sided skirmishes. So far we had not met any sure-enough fighting Yankees."[13] Some decided to find a little entertainment instead of sleep. Lt. H. C. Dawson of the First Arkansas Mounted Rifles called to one of his men to get his fiddle "and let's have a little dance and fun; it may be the last time we will ever dance together." Dawson was correct; by the close of the following day, both would be dead.[14]

McCulloch and Price were under a great deal of pressure to keep their coalition army together, drive the Federals from southwest Missouri, and score another victory as glorious as Manassas. To Major General Price, it was an opportunity to begin "reclaiming" the state for the secessionist cause. For Brigadier General McCulloch, it was a chance to end the Union threat to northwest Arkansas and the Indian Territory, which he had been ordered to defend. The grimly determined men in the Southern ranks, low on supplies and ammunition, hunkered down in the dismal rain on August 9, unaware that just a few hours later, they would get their wish to meet "fighting Yankees." Then it would be a storm of lead, not rain, that would fall on Wilson's Creek.

12
LYON'S ADVANCE

Brig. Gen. Nathaniel Lyon's 4,200-man command marching
west from Springfield in the early evening of August 9 con-
sisted of three brigades (the Second Brigade was with Col.
Franz Sigel). The First Brigade, commanded by Maj. Samuel
Sturgis, boasted some of the most reliable soldiers in the Army
of the West. It included a four-company battalion of regulars
led by Capt. Joseph Plummer, Lyon's West Point classmate;
two companies of the Second Missouri Infantry; two mounted
companies (one from the Second Kansas Infantry and one
from the regular cavalry); and Company F, Second US Artillery
(James Totten's Battery). The Third Brigade was made up of
the First Missouri Infantry, Lt. John DuBois's ad-hoc Regular
Army Battery, and another four-company battalion of regulars
under Capt. Frederick Steele. Volunteers composed the third
and largest brigade, with the First Iowa, First Kansas, and
Second Kansas Infantry regiments.

Frederick Steele, a captain in the Regular Army in the spring of 1861, led a battalion of regulars at Wilson's Creek.

The Federal commander hoped to surprise the enemy along Wilson's Creek. To that end, he issued orders for cannon wheels to be covered in blankets, infantry accoutrements to be arranged so that there would be no "clink" from bayonets or tin cups, and no music played. To further ensure the column's security, Lyon opted not to march from Springfield on the Telegraph (or Wire) Road. Although it was the most direct route to the Southern camp, it was also the road that Brig. Gen. Ben McCulloch would expect an enemy to take. Instead, the Federal column trudged west from Springfield for about six miles, turned south, and headed cross-country toward the enemy encampment. The men were cautioned to talk in low tones, although "there wasn't much talking," remembered one Iowa soldier, for "the men believed deadly work was in prospect and were silent as they pondered over the future."[1]

"About every other man was sure he would never come out alive," wrote a Kansan, so they were exchanging messages to be sent to the folks at home or giving away their personal possessions to those not as certain of their doom. But not every soldier was silently contemplating his fate. "It would never have been mistaken for a funeral procession," wrote Albert Greene. Officers moved back and forth along the column, chatting, visiting, telling jokes, and "having a good time generally." In the initial stages of the march, some men burst into song, including their own parody of an old Methodist hymn.[2] In the ranks of the First Kansas, "bets were freely offered and taken that the rebels would run as they always had done previously."[3]

Finally, about 1:00 a.m., "after many unaccountable delays on the road," as one regular complained, the tired troops halted for a brief rest only about two miles from their target. Robert Friedrich of the Second Kansas remembered "silently dropping down on the dew-damp prairie grass without blankets or covering," and sleeping on their arms until just before daylight. Friedrich recalled that he slept soundly "and resumed the march with all a boy's enthusiasm, in anticipation of a big time, and an opportunity to fire all the cartridges I choose."[4] Regular recruit John Dailey made a comfortable bed using his blanket and a fence rail for a pillow. "We'll look like this [prostrate on the ground] when McCulloch gets through with us," a fellow regular grimly joked.[5] Iowan private Eugene F. Ware was asleep in "from five to ten seconds and slept deliciously." Ware had made up his mind that he was certainly not going to be killed and would need all his strength to escape the dreaded Southern cavalry. He believed that the "anxiety which novelists describe, and the wakefulness on the eve of battle, are creatures I presume of the imagination of the novelists respectively, who were never there."[6]

Others were far more solemn and apprehensive about the upcoming fight. Even the commanding general had his misgivings. Lyon shared a blanket with Maj. John Schofield, his chief of staff, who was close to the general and well qualified to judge his mood. The general was unusually quiet. Schofield felt his commander "seemed greatly depressed, and except to give orders, hardly uttered a word." Although he was determined to fight a battle on unequal terms and whatever the cost, against the advice of some subordinates and superiors, Brigadier General Lyon still seemed to feel abandoned by Maj. Gen. John C. Fremont and believed he was "the intended victim of a deliberate sacrifice to another's ambition."[7]

About 4:00 a.m., as the eastern sky began to grow light, Lyon's force was quietly awakened, without drum or bugle, and fell into ranks. As the march continued, Capt. C. C. Gilbert's company of regulars was thrown out as skirmishers. The advancing Federals not only had to worry about Southern pickets but also had to contend with the terrain. "Our pathway was very rough and broken," wrote Kansas captain Joseph Cracklin, and "covered with loose and detached portions of rock, which made the marching very laborious."[8]

Soon the struggling Federals encountered the enemy—not alert pickets that should have warned the Southern army, but hungry foragers—men who had left camp in search of breakfast. The startled Southerners managed to get off a few shots at Lyon's regulars and then quickly fell back to their commands. Lyon formed a line of battle, with the Second Missouri on the right, Captain Plummer's Regular Battalion on the left, and Captain Totten's Battery in the center, and continued to press south. They soon reached the small farmhouse of Elias B. "E. B." Short, whose family was preparing to have breakfast. One of the Federals noted that the Short children "looked with surprise at so many hunters all dressed alike, and evidently wondered what particular game we were in search of." Short and his family, correctly assuming that a fierce fight was in the making, hurriedly packed what belongings they could and fled the area.[9]

Thanks to the reports of their foraging soldiers, at least some officers in Brigadier General McCulloch's army were aware that something peculiar was afoot and that enemy forces were in the vicinity. Missouri doctor John Snyder was at the headquarters of Gen. James S. Rains (near Gibson's Mill, on the eastern side of Wilson's Creek) that morning, discussing the events of the night before, when a group of empty forage wagons thundered past, the drivers "yelling like Indians and urging their jaded teams to the top of their speed." A wagon master stopped before the pair and almost screamed at Rains

SAMUEL DAVIS STURGIS

Born in Pennsylvania in 1822, Sturgis graduated from the US Military Academy in 1846, thirty-second in his class of fifty-nine that included George McClellan, Thomas J. Jackson, George Stoneman, and George Pickett. Commissioned a brevet second lieutenant in the Second Dragoons, Sturgis was promoted to second lieutenant in 1847; while reconnoitering the Mexican Army just prior to the 1847 Battle of Buena Vista, he was captured and held for eight days before being released. He served at posts in California, Missouri, Kansas, and New Mexico and was promoted to first lieutenant in 1853. Sturgis saw action against the Apaches in New Mexico in 1854 and 1855 and was promoted to captain; he fought against the Cheyenne Indians in 1857 and the Kiowas and Comanches in 1860. In command of Fort Smith, Arkansas, when the Civil War began, Sturgis evacuated the post to avoid capture on April 23, 1861, taking with him valuable government property; subsequently, he was promoted to major. Sturgis joined Brig. Gen. Nathaniel Lyon's Army of the West in July 1861 and became a brigade commander; he assumed command of the army upon Lyon's death at the Battle of Wilson's Creek. Advanced to brigadier general of volunteers, Sturgis went east and participated in the Battle  of Second Manassas and led a division in the Antietam and Fredericksburg Campaigns. Later he returned to the Western Theater and was soundly defeated by Nathan Bedford Forrest at the Battle of Brice's Cross Roads, Mississippi, in June 1864; he did not return to the field for the remainder of the war. Brevetted major general for his role in the Battle of Fredericksburg, Sturgis continued to serve in the Regular Army following the Civil War. He was named colonel of the Seventh US Cavalry in 1869. After service at several western posts and at the Soldiers' Home, Sturgis retired in 1886 and died in Saint Paul, Minnesota, on September 28, 1889.

that he had gone to look for forage but had instead found Federals advancing "in full force."

Rains calmly ordered the doctor to go have a look, so Snyder mounted his horse and went to reconnoiter. "Memory will never permit the sight that met my astonished gaze then and there . . . to be dimmed or marred by the flight of years," he recalled. About a mile away marched columns of Federal infantry, with flags flying and musket barrels glistening in the early morning sun, accompanied by several pieces of artillery. As Snyder had seen only small numbers of enemy soldiers to that point in his military career, it appeared to him that the whole prairie was covered with men and cannon, and he admitted it was "a grand and exhilarating sight." He quickly returned to tell Rains what he had seen, and Rains ordered the doctor to report to Maj. Gen. Sterling Price. Snyder's horse moved across Wilson's Creek like a deer, and the doctor soon found himself at Price's headquarters, next to William B. Edwards's cabin.

What happened next is unclear. According to Snyder, Price came out of his tent, buttoning his suspenders, and took the physician's breathless report that twenty thousand Federals with at least one hundred cannon would be overlooking Price's headquarters in less than half an hour. Price quickly mounted his horse and rode off to set his troops in motion. Thomas L. Snead, the general's aide, gave a slightly different account of the events at the Edwards' cabin. He claimed that at dawn Price sent him to McCulloch's headquarters to find out when the army would march on Springfield. McCulloch decided to confer with Price in person, so at about 5:10 a.m. he and his adjutant, Col. James McIntosh, arrived at the Missourian's tent and sat down to breakfast with Price. Then, according to Snead, Dr. Snyder arrived to deliver his message. McCulloch, unconcerned, ordered the doctor to return to General Rains and tell him he would come to the front "directly." When a second messenger from Rains arrived at the Edwards farm about 5:30, the generals sprang into action. Price left to confer with Rains and sent orders to his other division commanders to form their men. McCulloch returned to his own headquarters to rouse his troops.[10]

Though McCulloch and Price were initially slow to respond to the crisis, other Southern officers acted decisively to deal

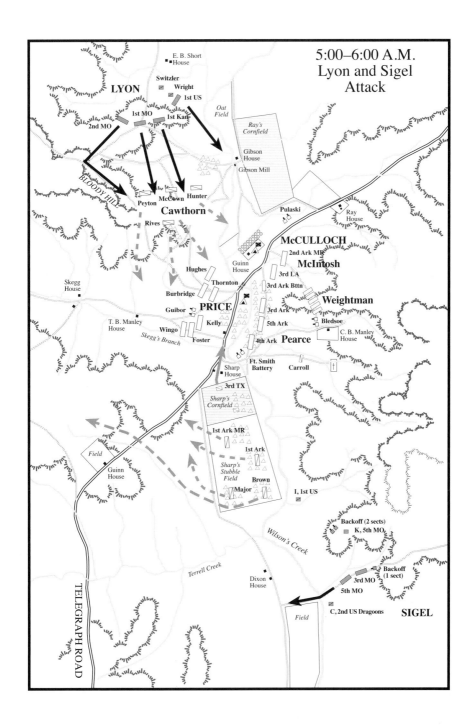

5:00–6:00 A.M.
Lyon and Sigel
Attack

E. B. Short House

LYON

Switzler
Wright
1st US
1st MO
1st Kans
2nd MO

Oat Field

Ray's Cornfield

Gibson House
Gibson Mill

McCown Hunter

Peyton

Cawthorn

Rives

Pulaski

Ray House

BLOODY HILL

McCULLOCH

2nd Ark MR

McIntosh

3rd LA

Skegg House

Hughes

Guinn House

3rd Ark Bttn

Thornton

Burbridge

Guibor

PRICE

3rd Ark

Weightman

T. B. Manley House

Wingo

Kelly

5th Ark

Bledsoe

C. B. Manley House

Foster

4th Ark

Pearce

Skegg's Branch

Sharp House

Ft. Smith Battery

Carroll

3rd TX

Sharp's Cornfield

1st Ark MR

Field

Guinn House

1st Ark

Sharp's Stubble Field

Brown

Major

I, 1st US

Wilson's Creek

Backoff (2 sects)
K, 5th MO

Terrell Creek

Dixon House

Backoff (1 sect)

3rd MO

5th MO

TELEGRAPH ROAD

Field

C, 2nd US Dragoons

SIGEL

Lt. Col. James McCown commanded the Second Cavalry Regiment, Eighth Division, Missouri State Guard, at Wilson's Creek.

with the Federals. Col. James Cawthorn—the commander of the twelve hundred cavalrymen of the Missouri State Guard's Eighth Division, camped at the northern end of the Wilson's Creek valley—had also heard the startling news brought by the foraging parties. He sent one of his regiments (about three hundred men under Col. Dewitt C. Hunter) to investigate. The State Guardsmen crested a rise near their camp and saw Lyon's men moving across the Short farm. Hunter quickly deployed his force on a ridge south of the Short farmhouse to slow the Federal advance and sent word to Cawthorn, who moved the other two regiments of his brigade into position to the south, on a high, flat rise that was soon christened "Bloody Hill."

Brigadier General Lyon was prepared to deal with Cawthorn's brave but hopelessly outnumbered horsemen. He positioned two of Captain Totten's guns in the center of a line of battle, supported by the First Missouri, with Captain Plummer's regulars on the left and the Second Missouri on the right. The remaining four guns of Totten's Battery were moved to the far right to enfilade the Southern line. When these troops were in place, Totten's Battery fired the first shots of the battle about 5:00 a.m., and the Federal line quickly advanced and drove Colonel Hunter's men from the ridge. The State Guardsmen fell back to join the rest of Cawthorn's brigade on Bloody Hill.

The men in the Federal ranks experienced a wide range of emotions during these opening minutes of Lyon's attack. A

Kansan believed that with the first shots, "the blood quickened its lazy pace—the sleepy eyes were opened; the wearied feet received new strength."[11] An unidentified private in Company G of the First Kansas wrote after the battle that although his regiment was in reserve at this point, when "Totten's dogs began to bark," the men were "startled" by the scream of shells. The roar of artillery and small arms, the thud of bullets, and the sight of the unit's first casualties made the men more than a little nervous. Bets made only a few hours before that the rebels would run "might have been [with]drawn without objection." However, in a strange transformation, and although the Kansans could see little of the action, the sight of thick clouds of musket smoke and the dull thud of artillery sparked an urge to enter the fight. One Kansan thought "there was no chance for my life, but as soon as the old cannon . . . made the earth shake, I forgot all fear."[12] The order "Kansas First to the front!" was met with "one good hearty cheer."[13] "I was pleased beyond measure," wrote Robert Friedrich of the Second Kansas, for here was an actual battle, and "they were going to let me be in it." Friedrich thought Brigadier General Lyon had "the most formidable and powerful army on earth," and he wondered at the "foolhardy audacity of the rebels" to challenge them.[14]

Before continuing his drive south against Colonel Cawthorn's Missouri State Guardsmen, Lyon made two crucial decisions. Fearing that the Southerners might move up the Wire Road and cut his force off from Springfield, he divided his small command, sending Colonel Plummer's three hundred US regulars and two companies of mounted Missouri Home Guards across to the east side of Wilson's Creek. As Lyon and the remainder of the army under his command pressed south, Plummer was instructed to move along the opposite bank and "carry forward the left flank of the attack." Lyon also brought forward the First Kansas Infantry and directed that regiment to fall in on the left flank of the battle line, joining the First and Second Missouri. He ordered most of the remainder of his units to move southwest, using farm roads, to outflank Cawthorn's line on Bloody Hill. The Kansans and Missourians pressed forward and easily pushed Cawthorn's small force down the southern slope of Bloody Hill. By 5:30 a.m., the leading elements of the Federal army had reached the crest of the broad, flat rise, where they halted to wait for those comrades who had been sent to outflank Cawthorn to return and extend the battle line.

13

Bloody Hill Earns Its Name

As the Union troops appeared on Bloody Hill, another small group of State Guardsmen attempted to slow Brig. Gen. Nathaniel Lyon's advance. About three hundred yards south of the hill's crest was the camp of the 284 members of Col. Benjamin Rives's First Cavalry Regiment, Fourth Division. Nineteen-year-old Lt. W. H. Ashby was roasting some green corn for breakfast when he heard the rattle of small arms. Ashby was not terribly concerned, as shooting was a "common habit among the unorganized assemblage." But as the scattered "popping" grew nearer and increased, Ashby became worried. Rives was concerned as well, for he sent an orderly to find Ashby and tell him to report to regimental headquarters. Ashby was ordered to select ten men from his company and ride forward to scout the cause of the firing. Ashby and his detachment rode off and covered less than half a mile when they blundered into the advancing Federals, only fifty feet away. Ashby instinctively drew his Colt revolver and "from pure lack of sense," as he described it, began blazing away at the enemy. But realizing the size of the Federal force, he quickly ordered a retreat. The Federals opened fire, but miraculously Ashby and his patrol escaped unharmed, except for one horse that was slightly wounded.

The young officer returned to find Rives and his men formed in line of battle. Ashby quickly made his report. "He asked me if I did not think he had better fall back," Ashby recalled, and the lieutenant said yes, "without any hesitation." Before the colonel could act, the Federals appeared and loosed another volley. This time the State Guardsmen were not so lucky. Lt. Col. A. J. Austin—Rives's second in command, who was listening to Ashby's report—took a bullet in the neck, toppled from his horse, and died almost instantly. Ashby was stunned. He was horrified by Austin's death but also thought "the whole proceeding unfair," as the Federals, "if they had any decency, would wait a few moments until we could get ourselves in position and compose our nerves for the fight." But Lyon would not wait, and Rives quickly ordered his men to retreat from Bloody Hill.[1]

But not every Southerner retreated in the face of the Federal advance. In fact, one small, resolute unit helped bring Lyon's triumphant advance to a halt on Bloody Hill and bought valuable time for the rest of Maj. Gen. Sterling Price's State Guardsmen to form ranks and advance to meet him.

On the east side of Wilson's Creek, near Brig. Gen. Ben McCulloch's headquarters, Capt. William E. Woodruff's Pulaski (Little Rock) Arkansas Battery waited. Unlike many other Southerners on the field, Woodruff's men were well-dressed and drilled militia soldiers. The unit was composed of the "elite of Little Rock" and sported uniforms of natty gray jackets and trousers trimmed in red. Ironically, Capt. James Totten, the Federal battery commander now facing them across Wilson's Creek, had trained Capt. "Billy" Woodruff and his men. Totten had commanded the garrison at the Little Rock Arsenal just before the war began and had lent his expertise in training Woodruff's new unit. When the Arkansas militia forces surrounded the arsenal in February 1861 and demanded its surrender, Totten withdrew, leaving his artillery behind. "As fate would have it," wrote Brig. Gen. Nicholas Pearce, Woodruff "was to win his first laurels in an artillery drill with their former instructor and with my guns that had formerly constituted Totten's battery."[2]

Woodruff's guns were sited in a strategic position astride the Telegraph Road, on high ground commanding both the major ford of Wilson's Creek and the creek valley. Woodruff's men, like so many others that morning, were finishing their breakfast of green corn when they heard a commotion and then saw the State Guardsmen retreating before the Federal advance. Woodruff prudently ordered his troops to their posts at the battery's four artillery pieces, and within a minute or two they watched an enemy battery, probably Totten's, unlimber on Bloody Hill and begin firing. The Arkansans went into battery as a second Federal artillery unit appeared on Bloody Hill. This second unit also began throwing rounds at Woodruff's men. The Federals managed to get off only three or four shots before the Pulaski Battery roared into action.

By simply being in the right place at the right time, the men of the Pulaski Battery were able to enfilade Lyon's line on Bloody Hill, forcing the Federal commander to turn his attention to the east and deal with the threat. This was not the only factor that governed Brigadier General Lyon's decision to halt his advance over Bloody Hill. He also opted to wait for the troops he had sent to outflank Col. James Cawthorn to arrive because he was unsure of the enemy's strength at the base of Bloody Hill. But clearly the harassing fire of the Arkansas guns helped stop the Federal drive and buy Price a few crucial minutes to form his units in line of battle and move them up Bloody Hill to oppose the Union advance. Although the battery might not have done "great execution," as Dr. W. A. Cantrell, a

THE BATTLE-FIELD OF WILSON'S CREEK AS SEEN FROM BEHIND PEARCI

Panoramic view of the Wilson's Creek battlefield, circa 1883.

fellow Arkansan, believed, historians would agree with Cantrell's other claims that Capt. Woodruff's battery was "the main stay in the contest" and "did signal service."[3]

But such an advantage came at great cost. The effective counter-battery fire of the Federal guns felled three men in the Pulaski Battery, including young lieutenant Omer Weaver, who was struck by a Federal solid shot that broke his right arm and crushed his chest. The "brave and chivalrous boy" died a short time later. A fellow Little Rock resident wrote just after the battle that Weaver's loss "is generally deplored, and we, who knew him best, most sincerely mourn the sudden termination of a life so full of promise."[4]

By 6:30 a.m., all of Lyon's units had been reunited, and the Federals had established a respectable line of battle on Bloody Hill. The morning had begun well for the Union general. His force had pushed all opposition aside with few casualties, and his men were now in a very good defensible position on a broad, high, flat plain. But thanks to the quick thinking of Woodruff and the Missouri State Guard commanders, Brigadier General Lyon's advance had stalled. Dealing with the Missourians and Arkansans had cost him valuable time and forced him to deploy. Lyon and his men could not see to the base of Bloody Hill, convincing the general that abandoning the high ground and plunging ahead with his whole force into the unknown

THE EAST SIDE OF THE CREEK — SEE MAP, PAGE 290. FROM PHOTOGRAPHS.

would be unwise. He had lost the initiative, and his men would be fixed in place on the hill for the remainder of the battle. They would soon face the might of the eager and motivated Missouri State Guard.

After being interrupted at breakfast by Dr. John Snyder, Major General Price and Brigadier General McCulloch had hurried off to form their commands. Price first issued orders to his division commanders to form their men and then had tried to ride north to meet Gen. James S. Rains. He rode into the advancing Federal line instead, so he quickly turned to rallying Colonel Cawthorn's disorganized brigade at the base of Bloody Hill. Much as Lyon was doing on Bloody Hill, Price fed the arriving units into a growing line of battle. Soon he had a formidable force—perhaps two thousand infantrymen and dismounted cavalrymen, along with Capt. Henry Guibor's State Guard Battery— ready to oppose the Federals on the hill's crest.

Considering that most Missourians were just waking up or cooking breakfast when the battle began, the quick response of the State Guard units was admirable. Most units, like Joseph Mudd's company, quickly formed ranks and "certainly lost not a minute" marching to the fight.[5] Missouri State Guardsman Thomas Bacon recalled that the Guardsmen had cooked their ration of coarsely ground wheat in skillets when Col. John Q. Burbridge calmly told Bacon's captain to form his men immediately. The cook broke the bread into pieces and distributed it, so "with a piece of bread in one hand and a gun in the other we formed in line." The company butcher, in the act of slaughtering a sheep, did not wash the blood off his hands, but instead rushed for his weapon and fell into line. "Our fighting men had come to stay," Bacon proudly said.

That is not to say that men on both sides were without fear when they first went into action. Although inspired by Captain Woodruff's pounding of the Federals on Bloody Hill, the State Guardsmen realized that the moment of truth had arrived. When Bacon and his comrades encountered a dead soldier, they were "profoundly influenced" by the sight. "The ghastly hopelessness of his filmy eyes inspired us with sudden horror," Bacon remembered years later. When he spied Federal skirmishers in Bloody Hill, Bacon "swallowed a lump in my throat and resigned the hope of life."[6]

Fortunately, the State Guardsmen would not have to face Brigadier General Lyon's entire command initially. Rather than drive recklessly off Bloody Hill, Lyon decided to send only a "reconnaissance in force" consisting of the First Missouri and six companies of the First Kansas forward from his main battle line to probe beyond the crest. The two units soon marched away from each other and would fight independently. Price and the Missouri units he had been able to form into line of battle waited on the south slope of Bloody Hill for the Federal advance. With fingers on the triggers of shotguns, hunting rifles, and smoothbore muskets, the Missourians held their fire as the Federals came within range. Volleys shattered the morning air, and the fighting began in earnest.

While their comrades tested the Missouri State Guard, the other four companies of the First Kansas, under Maj. John Halderman, supported Totten's Battery. Exposed and under the intense fire of Woodruff's battery, Halderman ordered his men to lie down, but as the commanding officer, Halderman could not join his men without sacrificing his honor and reputation. More than forty years after the battle, one of J. M. Lindley's vivid memories of the fight was of Halderman sitting on his large, iron-gray horse amid the fire, where it seemed he could not escape death. Lindley also noted that Halderman encouraged his soldiers by telling them that "any man who was killed there that day would go straight to heaven." One of the Kansas sergeants, an English veteran who had lost an eye in the Crimean War, said later that if Halderman could survive the storm, he would risk his other eye, so instead of lying down he rested on his knee and discharged his weapon "to good advantage." When Halderman saw what the sergeant was doing, he motioned him to lie down as ordered. Halderman's bold action inspired his Kansans, but in reality, he was not all that self-assured. "I would have signed a million-dollar note," he admitted later, "if the truth were known, for the privilege of hugging that ground for a little while."[7] Mercifully, Lyon soon ordered the remainder of the First Kansas forward to help their beleaguered comrades, and Halderman quite literally dodged the bullet.

As the fighting intensified, ready units of the State Guard took their places at Bloody Hill and extended the Southern line of battle westward. Eventually the momentum shifted back in favor of the Southerners. The six hundred infantrymen (two regiments) of State Guard general James McBride's Seventh Division fell in on the far left of the Southern line. Ordered to support Captain Guibor's Battery, they instead moved past the battery and began to advance alone up Bloody Hill. One State Guardsmen noticed that McBride's men ran up the hill "bent double, partly to run uphill more easily, and principally to remain as close to the ground as possible."[8] Although potentially disastrous for the Missourians, McBride's advance actually worked to Major General Price's advantage. He not only pushed around Brigadier General Lyon's First Missouri Infantry, but as the State Guardsmen also marched forward, units from other State Guard divisions joined in an uncoordinated charge up Bloody Hill.

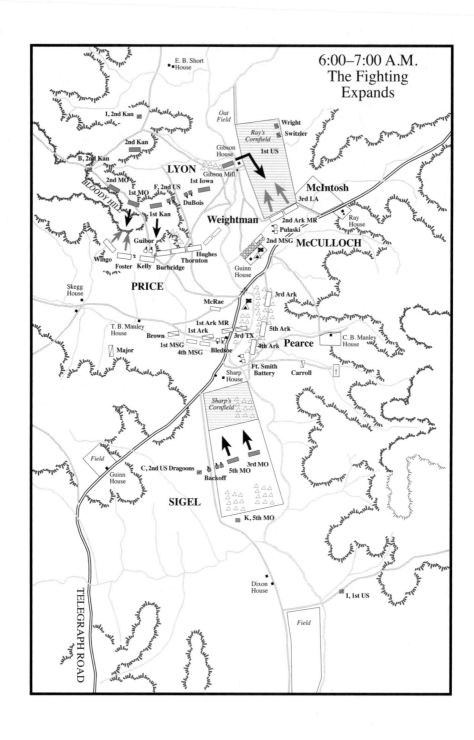

Although the First Missouri and First Kansas made a stubborn stand as long as possible, gradually the small Federal
presence was outflanked and forced to retire. The First
Missouri withdrew first, forcing the Kansans to do likewise. By
7:30 a.m., the two regiments had returned to the battle line on
the crest of Bloody Hill. To counter the Southern advance, Lyon
ordered the Second Kansas forward from their reserve position. To buy time until they arrived, he told Col. George Deitzler
and his First Kansas to launch a bayonet charge. In the confusion, only two full companies and a portion of a third of the
regiment made the charge, but they accomplished their mission
and forced the Missourians to fall back. However, Deitzler was
severely wounded and his horse killed. The impetuous Kansans
also "soon found that their ardor was likely to cost them dear,"
for they were almost surrounded. Lyon ordered them to return
again to the crest.[9] Their charge and the arrival of the six hundred men of the Second Kansas forced Price to withdraw his
Guardsmen to the base of Bloody Hill. By about 8:00 a.m., the
first Southern assault on the hill had ended.

Although the fighting had been fierce on Bloody Hill, and
neither side had won a significant advantage, the Southerners
had already enjoyed dramatic success on another part of the
battlefield.

14
THE CORNFIELD

Capt. Joseph Plummer, in command of three companies of the First US Infantry and a company of regular recruits, had been ordered to cross Wilson's Creek and secure the Federal left flank just after Brig. Gen. Nathaniel Lyon's encounter with Col. Dewitt C. Hunter's State Guard cavalry. Accompanied by two local mounted Home Guard companies, Plummer worked his way with some difficulty across the creek near John Gibson's house and mill.[1] Unlike most of Lyon's units, the regular battalion was a mixture of veterans and new recruits. Although most men in the First US companies had several months or years of peacetime service, the company of recruits was made up of green soldiers who had enlisted only weeks before the battle. Fortunately, the officers and noncommissioned officers in Plummer's command were experienced, and collectively the regular battalion enjoyed better discipline than the volunteer regiments. Lyon had chosen the right men for this assignment—the professional soldiers were expected to be more reliable under fire than the ninety-day enlistees.

The regulars crossed to the east side of the creek, and on the opposite bank they found a "jungle" of willows and reeds and had to push and pull each other through the morass, their shoes filling with water and sand. Once through that obstacle, they began marching quickly to the south. They entered John Ray's cornfield about 6:30 a.m., moving as quickly as possible through the ripe corn. Somewhere near the middle of the field, Plummer noticed Capt. William Woodruff's Pulaski Battery just to the south, firing into his Union comrades on Bloody Hill. Aiming to silence the guns "should the opportunity offer," Plummer quickly pushed his men in that direction.

Unfortunately for the regulars, the Southerners were moving swiftly as well to guarantee that Plummer would never lay claim to the Pulaski Battery. Woodruff himself spied the approaching regulars and quickly sent an appeal for support to Brig. Gen. Ben McCulloch's headquarters. Concerned about the situation on other parts of the battlefield, McCulloch decided not to go to Ray's Cornfield in person; instead, he sent Col. James McIntosh, who took his own Second Arkansas Mounted Rifles, the Third Louisiana, and Col. Dandridge McRae's Arkansas Battalion—a force of more than 1,300 men. Although McRae's Battalion was soon detached to support Woodruff's Battery, the remaining 1,100 Arkansans and Louisianans were more than enough to handle Plummer's small force. McIntosh's men soon sighted the rail fence that marked the southern edge of the cornfield, with Plummer's men just on the other side. He quickly deployed his regiments, and eventually his men moved forward to take cover behind the fence.

Captain Plummer reacted quickly as well. He soon realized that he had been caught in an open field by a rapidly growing enemy force, that he would have difficulty crossing the rail fence, and that he would have to cause as much damage as he could before the full weight of the enemy could be brought

The John Ray House at Wilson's Creek, circa 1883.

to bear. Plummer ordered his men to open fire when only two of the Louisiana companies had deployed. The fence was lined with briars and weeds, and beyond it was brush and foliage; at first the regulars fired blindly, some of their rounds finding targets, but most being lost in the fence or underbrush. Even worse, at least some of Plummer's men were armed with smoothbore muskets firing "buck and ball" (one large bullet and three smaller buckshot). Normally a lethal weapon at close range, the poor visibility negated its effectiveness, and after firing three rounds, "the guns were useless, being foul," one regular complained.

Despite these disadvantages, Plummer's men kept up their fire. They abandoned the precise drill they had been taught on the parade ground, breaking ranks to give each man room to load and fire. Each "assumed a position to his liking—most of them on their knees," some even lying down flat to fire and rolling on their backs to reload. Plummer himself paced behind his men, shouting encouragement, as bullets "rattled in the cornfield like drops of rain driven by violent winds." Lt. Henry Clay Wood and Plummer's other subordinates followed his example, instructing their men how to aim, telling them to ignore the wounded, and trying to keep up their courage. The regulars were standing fast amid the deafening roar of battle and the curses and moans of the wounded.

Despite their best efforts, Plummer's "little band" was growing smaller, suffering heavy casualties. They were gradually being outflanked as well. Colonel McIntosh had not planned to do so, but because he had such a large number of troops to bring into line, his companies eventually filled the space in front of Captain Plummer and then began to wrap around the eastern side of the cornfield. When companies of the Third Louisiana reached the Federal left flank, Plummer's men had to face enemy fire from two directions. It was only a question of time before even his well-trained regulars would be forced to give way.

Plummer had few options. With no sign of reinforcements and no desire to humiliate himself by retreating, but also recognizing that his force would collapse if the enemy charged, he opted to charge first. He called for his bugler, but the musician was dead. He then tried to pass the word and lead the assault, but a bullet shattered one of his ribs. Soon hoarse from shouting and weak from loss of blood, Plummer was content to urge his men to keep firing.

McIntosh's men were suffering as well from "a deadly fire." Pvt. Placide Bossier of Company G, Third Louisiana, "a gentleman of wealth and position," was one of the casualties in the cornfield fight, severely wounded by a shot to the neck. The bullet cut Bossier's throat nearly in two as it exited the opposite side. Pvt. Paul Bossier saw his "best and truest friend" on the ground, so he threw down his gun, picked Placide up in his arms, and with the help of a comrade moved him into the brush. "I saw I could not help him," Paul Bossier wrote later. "He tried to speak but could not," so Bossier took up his weapon and went back to work.

J. A. Prudhomme of the same company loved Placide "as a brother" and was also at his side. He heard the wounded man whisper that he was suffocating, but Prudhomme could not stay to watch his friend die. He bade Private Bossier goodbye, pressed his hand, and promised to avenge him. "I saw from his eyes that he understood me," Prudhomme said. Bossier beckoned for his canteen, told Prudhomme to go, and died about ten minutes later before the surgeon could reach him. Prudhomme was certain that he met death "like a man and a christian [sic]." Paul Bossier believed that he "died bravely, and prepared to meet his God." Prudhomme dutifully cut a lock of the soldier's hair and took his prayer book to send home to Bossier's mother and sisters. In a battle filled with many poignant deaths, Bossier's was certainly one of the most moving.

Despite such casualties in Colonel McIntosh's ranks, the regulars were weakening. With Captain Plummer unable to launch his own attack, McIntosh decided to begin a charge of his own to drive the enemy off. Although he rode to tell the Louisianans of his plan (shouting "over the fence and at them, Boys," according to one source), apparently he did not adequately brief his own company commanders, for when the charge was made, only about half of the Second Arkansas followed him. Even so, about nine hundred of the Southern force, a more than adequate number, surged across the fence and into the cornfield "with a loud cheer, or rather yell," and Plummer's battalion dissolved.[2]

The regulars withdrew in reasonably good order back through Ray's cornfield, but not everyone heard the command to retreat. Lt. Henry Wood's company of recruits stood steadfastly blazing away at the attacking enemy until some of his men pointed out to the young officer that the rest of the battalion had abandoned them. About the same time, Plummer rode up and ordered Wood's men to the rear; otherwise, Wood wrote, "I think we should have stayed, to be planted there, or perhaps captured." Wood was later awarded the Medal of Honor for his bravery in the cornfield that morning.

The regulars withdrew back through the cornfield, and the "terrible conflict of small-arms," as Brigadier General McCulloch described it, was over. Although the fight in Ray's cornfield had lasted less than an hour, the fighting had been intense, and casualties had been high on both sides. The three companies of the First US took 225 men into action that morning and lost 9 killed, 27 wounded, and 7 missing. The recruit company had 66 men in the action and suffered 10 killed, 25 wounded, and 2 missing, or nearly half of the battalion's 80 casualties. Although Lieutenant Wood felt the regulars could have remained longer, Captain Plummer's men had done all that could be expected and had lost more than a quarter of their strength.[3] The regular recruits in particular had performed well, suffering more than 50 percent casualties. Colonel McIntosh's force had also fought with bravery and had lost approximately 100 in killed and wounded.

Flushed with success, the Southerners followed Plummer's men and pushed deep into Ray's cornfield. However, over on Bloody Hill, Lt. John V. DuBois and Capt. Gordon Granger noticed Plummer's predicament. Supposedly exclaiming, "Oh, my God! See those Regulars over there!" Granger ordered DuBois to turn his guns and lay down a covering fire as Plummer's men withdrew back across Wilson's Creek. Although DuBois believed he caused "great slaughter," in fact the Federal guns caused few casualties. The Southerners were driven back in some disorder by the intense artillery fire, but during their retreat they practiced "Zouave" tactics.[4]

"We were too good Zouaves," wrote Prudhomme of the Third Louisiana, "for at every shot, every man of the Regiment dropped, and as soon as the ball or bomb had passed or exploded, they got up and started." But the rain of iron that DuBois delivered had done its work; he had stopped the pursuit of Plummer and forced the Southerners to retreat, with the Third Louisiana split into three separate groups.

With the Federal drive on the east side of Wilson's Creek decisively halted, the Southern commanders could now turn their entire attention to Brigadier General Lyon and Col. Franz Sigel. Unfortunately for the Federal commanding general, before the morning was over, one more Federal column would be broken and driven from the battlefield.

15
THE SHARP FARM

Col. Franz Sigel's brigade left Springfield at 6:30 p.m., August 9, with orders to gain the rear of the enemy camp and block any retreat as Brig. Gen. Nathaniel Lyon struck the opposite or northern end of the encampment.

The German colonel took with him two infantry regiments (the Third and Fifth Missouri), an artillery battery of six pieces, and two companies of mounted troops (one regular dragoon and a regular cavalry company)—a total of about 1,200 men. They initially moved south and then turned southwest toward Wilson's Creek. "The night was dark and cloudy," wrote acting Second Lt. Otto Lademann of the Third Missouri, and "occasionally we had light showers of rain, some thunder and lightning intermixed." Like Lyon's column, the men marched in silence. Apart from the occasional barking farm dog, the only sounds heard were the clanking of arms and rumbling of the artillery carriages. About 11 p.m.—again, like Lyon's column—the men halted for a rest. At 2 a.m., they resumed their push forward.

This was not the same brigade that had performed so well at Carthage. Although Sigel had persuaded each company of the Fifth Missouri Infantry to remain with him, about four hundred members of the Third Missouri Infantry, veterans of the July battle, had already been mustered out. Now perhaps two hundred "insufficiently drilled" recruits joined the same number of veterans in the regiment's ranks. Far worse, most of the artillerymen who had saved the day for him at Carthage had gone home as well. Now infantry recruits from the Third Missouri manned the pieces and handled the artillery horses— not necessarily a detriment, except that these men had only a few days' instruction. Finally, about two-thirds of the brigade's officers had been discharged; in fact, some companies had no officers at all. In reality, the most critical mission of the battle had been assigned to the smallest and least prepared part of the Federal army.

Thanks to the services of local guides and the alertness of Colonel Sigel's men (who had arrested every civilian on the road and captured a large number of Southern foragers), by 5:30 a.m. the brigade slipped undetected into position on a high ridge overlooking Wilson's Creek and the farm of Joseph Sharp at the southern end of Brig. Gen. Ben McCulloch's encampment. Below them and parallel to the creek was a large, rectangular stubble field; farther to their right (north) was a smaller, square cornfield and Sharp's farmhouse and outbuildings. "At our feet in the misty valley of Wilson's creek was a large encampment of Confederate cavalry still enjoying their sweet morning slumbers," except for some cooks preparing breakfast, recalled Lademann. Sigel deployed four of his artillery pieces on the commanding rise, hidden by brush and guarded by the company of regular cavalry. The rest of Sigel's infantry, the dragoon company, and the other two guns moved on to the south to locate a crossing of Wilson's Creek.

When the sound of musketry from Lyon's attack reached Sigel, he ordered his guns to open fire and present "morning compliments" to the Southerners. "Gracious, how the boys tumbled out of their blankets," noted Lademann. Although Sigel's untrained artillerymen caused few casualties, the fire from his guns generated many psychological casualties in the Southern ranks. C. C. Woods was one of the Southern cavalrymen camped on the Sharp farm. A State Guardsman attached to Col. William B. Brown's First Cavalry Regiment, Sixth Division, Woods had slept soundly the night before the battle. The usual noises of camp had awakened him about sunrise. After caring for his horse, Woods walked to the campfire where "Uncle Stephen," his unit's African American cook, was preparing breakfast. One of his officers was lying on a camp bed close by, and just as Woods greeted him, they heard the roar of a cannon to the north. Woods remarked that possibly "the ball had opened," but before the officer could reply, there was "a fearful crash and roar" from Sigel's guns, and both knew that the fight had indeed started.

"It is needless to say that the regiment did not form exactly in that place," Woods remembered. "We were personally rather expeditious in arranging our horse and mounting." As they rode off with "a regretful glance at the untasted coffee and the smoking breakfast," they noticed that they were alone—everyone else had already fled. "The confusion was very great," Woods said, and when his unit reached the Wire Road, they found it filled with wagons and fugitives, mainly camp followers and unarmed men "who seemed to have suddenly remembered important engagements in Arkansas and were haunted with the fear of being late."[1] Not all the 2,450 Southerners surprised by Sigel on the Sharp farm reacted the same way. Some fled and never returned to the fighting; others, like Woods, maintained unit cohesion, retreated, and came back, while most, even if dispersed, eventually rallied and returned to the fight.

Colonel Sigel left his guns on the ridge, rode south to the Wilson's Creek ford, and caught up with the rest of his column.

Facing practically no opposition thanks to the effective artillery bombardment, Sigel's men turned north, crossed Terrell Creek, and moved along a farm road on the western side of Sharp's large stubble field.

But not all the Southerners had been driven off the Sharp farm. In fact, several hundred were rallying near the Sharp farm buildings to the north and near the northeastern corner of the cornfield. Sigel estimated their numbers at 2,500 to 3,000, so about 6:30 a.m. he halted the column about halfway along the stubble field fence and sent word back to the ridge to bring the rest of his cavalry and artillery down to reunite the brigade. About 7:00 a.m., with the artillery reunited, Sigel formed a line of battle across the stubble field. A twenty-minute or half-hour artillery bombardment, a "lively cannonade," dispersed the rallied enemy. An eyewitness reported that Sigel's canister rounds inspired great awe: "I never saw such scattering of shot as they bounded along," Capt. A. V. Rieff noted, "raising the dust. It beat any shot-gun I ever saw."[2] At about 8:00 a.m., the Federals marched north into the front yard of the Sharp house.

For Sigel, the morning had gone extremely well. He had dispersed a large part of the Southern army with a minimum of casualties and had taken about one hundred prisoners. His troops had maintained order and discipline, their morale was high, and they were now in position blocking the Wire Road—the major enemy retreat route. But as with Lyon, Sigel's initial success would soon evaporate in the face of determined Southern opposition.

Following their victory in Ray's cornfield and their subsequent retreat under fire from Lt. John DuBois's battery, the Third Louisiana Infantry had split into three segments. The regiment's officers, including Lt. Col. Samuel Hyams, set about rallying their commands. Hyams soon encountered McCulloch, who had just observed the crisis at the Sharp farm and was on his way back to his headquarters. Determined to deal

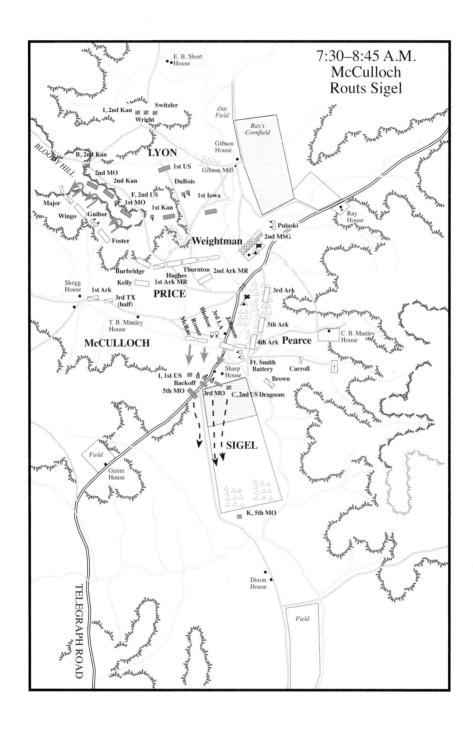

with Sigel, McCulloch grabbed two of the regiment's rallied companies, ordered Hyams to follow with any other available men, and sent word to Col. James McIntosh to bring help as well. McIntosh soon arrived, took command from Hyams, and led his detachment toward the Sharp farm. In all, about four hundred members of the regiment moved to oppose Sigel, plus a group of about seventy Missouri State Guardsmen who followed the Louisianans. After crossing Wilson's Creek, the cool and unemotional McCulloch halted several times to observe Sigel's position through his field glasses. Satisfied, he turned in the saddle, waved his hand to his men, and simply said, "Come on!"

Brigadier General McCulloch's forthcoming attack would receive help from a number of quarters, including Colonel Sigel himself. The Federal colonel had not only halted at the Sharp house rather than pushing forward to meet Brigadier General Lyon, but he had deployed his men poorly. Rather than arrange the entire brigade in line of battle, Sigel kept most of his infantry on either side of the Wire Road, closed up in "column of companies" (an arrangement best suited for movement, not combat, as only the lead company in each column could safely fire). He deployed only one battalion (250 men) of his mixed veteran-recruit Third Missouri Infantry in line of battle. He arranged his six artillery pieces to fire on Bloody Hill, but they were located dangerously close to the edge of a steep bluff that led down to Skegg's Branch, an east-west tributary of Wilson's Creek. In the words of acting second lieutenant Lademann, it was a "clumsy tactical formation" that made his men "a very good artillery target." To make matters worse, although Sigel correctly placed his mounted men to guard either flank, both companies either moved out of supporting distance or into fenced areas that made a quick response difficult.

Despite his tactical dispositions, by 8:30 a.m. Sigel was still confident of victory. He began to notice large numbers of Southern troops moving to the south, away from the fighting, along the ridge where he had started his bombardment. Some unarmed stragglers even walked down the Wire Road and into his waiting troops. The heavy firing on Bloody Hill had nearly ceased, leading him to believe that Lyon's attack had been successful. Although he had had no contact with Lyon, Sigel probably believed that now all he had to do was hold his place, blocking the Wire Road, bag any retreating Southerners,

Dr. Samuel Melcher served with Sigel's Brigade and helped recover the body of General Lyon from the Wilson's Creek battlefield.

and wait for Lyon to push south from Bloody Hill and link up with his brigade. In his mind, there was really no need to deploy his men and risk friendly fire casualties as Lyon's men drew near. He did employ two precautions: he kept an inadequate force of skirmishers out in front of the brigade and shifted four of his guns to fire up the Wire Road.

Soon the skirmishers returned to the main body with reports that troops were approaching on the Wire Road. Dr. Samuel Melcher, surgeon of the Fifth Missouri Infantry, had no casualties to treat, so he rode down the road as well. He returned to say that although "it was smoky, and objects at a distance could not be seen very distinctly," he saw a large body of men coming from the direction where they had heard Lyon's guns. "They look like the First Missouri [Iowa]," Melcher reported. Melcher's observation made some sense; the approaching soldiers were dressed in gray (as Sigel's men were), and about half of the First Iowa Infantry, serving under

Lyon, were dressed in gray. Sigel and his regimental commanders cautioned their men not to fire, but to be certain, Sigel also sent a corporal forward to challenge the approaching body and had one of his color-bearers wave the Stars and Stripes. The Union corporal soon encountered McCulloch himself. The Federal raised his musket to shoot the Southern commander, only to be shot in the head by a nearby Louisianan. Still alive, McCulloch ordered his men forward.

At the same moment, Brig. Gen. Nicholas Pearce was standing near the four-gun Fort Smith Battery. Although Pearce had placed the battery in position that morning on high ground overlooking Wilson's Creek and the Sharp house to guard against any Federal movements against the Southern right and rear, the area afforded poor visibility, and Capt. John Reid's artillerymen had little to do. Now, however, with Colonel Sigel's advance across the Sharp farm, the Arkansan guns were ideally located opposite Sigel's right flank. Even so, Pearce wasted valuable time trying to sort out whether Sigel's men were friend or foe. The general had apparently watched the Federals enter the Sharp farm, but he was unconvinced that enemy forces could be in his rear and was certain that these were friendly troops. One of Pearce's staff members, examining the scene with field glasses, was equally positive that they were the enemy.

Pearce ordered Capt. Tom Jefferson and Col. Emmett MacDonald of his staff to reconnoiter. Jefferson rode up to the Sharp house and demanded to know what command that was. One of Sigel's men pointed his musket at the officer and demanded his surrender. Jefferson promptly complied. MacDonald, seeing Jefferson's predicament, turned and escaped back to Pearce. By that time, Pearce later claimed, he had already surveyed the scene with his field glasses and seen the Federal color-bearer waving his flag. Finally convinced that the gray-clad troops were the enemy, Pearce turned to Reid, the battery's commander, and ordered him to open fire.[3]

Worse yet for the Federals, Capt. Hiram Bledsoe's Missouri State Guard battery, located across Skegg's Branch just north of Sigel's position, joined in the barrage. Now Sigel's men were under artillery fire from front and flank.

Although two of Sigel's guns responded, it mattered little, as the Louisianans surged forward and fired a volley point-blank into the Federals. Fortunately for the Southerners, thanks to Sigel's arrangement, they faced a relatively small force of only four guns and 250 men of the Third Missouri formed in line of battle. McCulloch's concentrated small-arms fire hit the Federals hard. "Consternation and frightful confusion" followed. Shaken by what they thought was friendly fire, some of the Federals who could actually return fire did so, while most simply stood mystified. At almost the same time, about seventy-five members of Dandridge McRae's Arkansas Battalion and an unknown number of State Guardsmen who had joined in Brigadier General McCulloch's attack crashed into the left flank of Sigel's brigade. Those Federals in line of battle dissolved, and the infantrymen and artillery drivers, horses, limbers, and caissons ran into the nearby columns of companies, creating what acting second lieutenant Lademann called "an indescribable mixture of men, horses, guns, and caissons."

"Col. Sigel's tactical skill having deprived us of every opportunity of employing our arms," Lademann bitterly wrote, "there was nothing left for us but to run, and run we did like good fellows." "If ever the Third Louisiana hold a regimental reunion," Lademann added, "they ought to pass a resolution of thanks to Col. Sigel for making their victory so very easy." Two of the Federal guns managed to escape, but four were captured. Ironically, some of the few casualties suffered by the Louisianans came not from Sigel's men but from "friendly fire" from the Fort Smith Battery, thanks to "the blunders of our officers," one Arkansas captain complained.[4]

Sigel's soldiers retreated from the battlefield in several different groups. Although a sizeable portion of his brigade was still intact (the Fifth Missouri had not fired a shot and had retreated in good order from the field), no members of the Second Brigade returned to the fight. Texas and Missouri cavalrymen pursuing Sigel caught up with him and a portion of his fugitives, and the Southerners quickly dispersed them and ran them down like "cowboys after jack rabbits." Sigel himself narrowly avoided capture and managed to arrive unharmed in Springfield about 4:30 p.m., before the remainder of the Federal army made it to town.[5] By day's end, Sigel lost about 166 men, or about 15 percent of his brigade's strength, most either wounded or captured, along with a fifth gun from his artillery battalion captured during the retreat.[6] By midmorning, with two Federal threats (Capt. Joseph Plummer and Colonel Sigel) turned back, Brigadier General McCulloch and Maj. Gen. Sterling Price were now free to concentrate their attention on Lyon on Bloody Hill.

16

THE STRUGGLE FOR BLOODY HILL CONTINUES

Despite the failure of the first Southern attack on Bloody Hill, by 9:00 a.m. Maj. Gen. Sterling Price and his subordinates had readied their men for another assault. Aided by the First and Second Arkansas Mounted Rifles and part of the Third Louisiana, the Missouri State Guardsmen surged up Bloody Hill once again.

The noise of the battle was impressive. Springfield residents could hear the boom of the cannon from Wilson's Creek like "the muttering of a thunder storm upon the horizon." As newspaper correspondent Franc Wilkie drew closer to the battle, he could hear the continuous roar of artillery, only now and then broken enough to hear individual guns. At times the earth shook "like Niagara." The noise "of a hundred thunderstorms mingled in one" or "a continuous discharge of huge firecrackers" would slacken for a moment, Wilkie explained, when perhaps a single gun could be heard, "then a half dozen in a succession so quick that each succeeding sound lapped on the preceding one; and then the lapping on would become indistinguishable, and the whole would be merged again in one terrific volume."[1]

Although some of the battle's participants had been under fire at Carthage, Forsyth, or Dug Springs, or long before in the Mexican War or the European revolutions of 1848, this was the first serious combat for the majority of men on both sides. Green soldiers unfamiliar with things military and laboring under the pressure of combat sometimes made odd comments or reacted in strange and unpredictable ways. While under fire from Southern artillery, one Kansan caught an iron shell or case shot fragment that had spent its force in the folds of his coat (all such rounds were made of iron rather than lead). The soldier remarked, "We've got 'em now; they're out of lead." Another member of the same regiment had his percussion cap pouch shot off his waist belt. "He made a terrible fuss about it," recalled a comrade, "fearing the battle would end in disaster in consequence." When a fellow soldier told the distressed warrior to simply take another cap pouch from one of the dead, the man did so and then "went coolly to loading and shooting as before."[2] Henry Blank of Company A, First Iowa, had been excused from duty as one of the army's butchers, but he shouldered his musket and insisted on going with his comrades to the battle. At one point, when the Iowans were driving off an enemy attack, Blank stepped forward ten or twelve paces in front of his company, deliberately cut a bush, and returned. When his captain questioned him, Blank explained that he wanted "a better sight at a devil over there."[3]

On the opposite side of Bloody Hill, Joseph A. Mudd of the State Guard also noticed some bizarre behavior among his comrades. Mudd watched as a man about thirty feet to his right suddenly dropped his gun, ran forward, and turning to the left, passed through Mudd's company. He threw himself on the ground a few feet in the rear, tore his clothing loose, and began searching for a wound. When comrades rushed to his side, he dramatically told them, "'Boys, tell my father I died fighting for my country." One of the men then picked out the bullet, which had penetrated just far enough to "keep its place until loosened by a slight movement of the finger"—hardly a fatal wound. The panicked soldier reaped many less-than-flattering remarks from his fellow soldiers for that performance. Mudd also noticed an aide to Gen. M. M. Parsons sitting on a dead horse, his back to the enemy, calmly eating his breakfast. The excitement of combat also caused new soldiers to grow careless while loading and firing their weapons. Mudd's comrade John Bowles, standing a little behind the fighting line, stepped up and fired his musket with the muzzle only three inches from Capt. William F. Carter's ear. The officer "faced about and gave the offender a sound scolding in which oaths were freely mingled," Mudd recalled. "I had never before heard swearing in battle, and was much shocked."[4]

Despite such diverting incidents, the men fighting on Bloody Hill realized amid the blood, screams, and death just how tenuous life could be. Early in the fight for Bloody Hill, the men of the First Iowa Infantry held the far left of Brig. Gen. Nathaniel Lyon's line. Only two companies were deployed as skirmishers, and the rest of the regiment remained inactive, their courage and resolve sorely tested by Southern musket and cannon fire. The men closest to the enemy were lying down. First Sgt. Hugh J. Campbell of Company A rose and walked over to a friend for a piece of chewing tobacco when he heard the call that one of his company had been killed. He returned and found Shelby Norman, "one of our best boys," on the ground with a large hole in his temple. The boy's eyes were closed, his breathing heavy and slow.

Norman had heard a soldier from a neighboring regiment derisively tell the Iowans: "Stand up! Don't be afraid of them." Norman, not willing to let anyone question his courage, sprang

Jeremiah V. Cockrell served as a lieutenant in Company E, Second Cavalry Regiment, Eighth Division, Missouri State Guard, at Carthage and Wilson's Creek.

to his feet and stood facing the fire. The next instant, he was cut down. Campbell put a coat under Norman's head and sent immediately for the regiment's surgeon. "One of the bravest and most faithful members of the company" was soon dead. Comrades recalled not only Norman's "dauntless and courageous spirit" but also the fact that earlier in the campaign, he had marched sixty miles barefoot, without a murmur, and without losing his place.[5]

Joseph McHenry of the same regiment rose on one knee to place a percussion cap on his musket when a bullet tore through his head, "scattering his blood and brains upon his comrades on either side of him. He was dead ere he reached the ground."[6] Tragically, deaths such as Norman and McHenry's were played out hundreds of times across the Wilson's Creek valley that morning.

Things were little better for the hundreds of wounded men who suffered from intense pain, loss of blood, and the lack of water and medical attention. Neither side had an organized hospital corps, so a wounded man had to make his way to the rear alone to find medical attention or persuade some of his comrades to help him there. After having their wounds dressed, however, some Union wounded returned to watch the battle. In other cases, wounded men at dressing stations were still close enough to the fighting to come under fire again.

Thomas Bacon of the Missouri State Guard was about to draw a bead on a Federal when he felt a "terrible blow."

He jumped up, his rifle flew from his hands, and he fell forward on all fours. Bacon moved to.the rear and sat down, but quickly realized he was sitting in a pool of his own blood from a wound in the right groin. Certain that he was mortally wounded, Bacon asked a nearby staff officer if he could go to the rear. When permission was granted, he staggered down the slope. As he moved, blood coursed into his shoes, and its odor filled the air. Bacon spied a hospital flag and found a group of wounded men lying on straw scattered on the ground. But he did not remain long at the impromptu dressing station. Soon canister shot from Col. Franz Sigel's guns ripped into the area, and Bacon was on the move again. He encountered other wounded men, looking like "stricken deer," and dead men whose "lips were blots of livid purple, their faces pallid yellow, their eyes like lamps gone out, their forms like fallen statues," and their blood flowing into Wilson's Creek. After Sigel's defeat, Bacon was able to return to the dressing station.[7]

First Sgt. Hugh Campbell of the First Iowa had a similar ordeal. When he was struck in the leg by a bullet, Campbell said he felt it immediately, although the wound was not painful. He found he could walk only slowly and with great difficulty. Stooping to try to stanch the bleeding with his handkerchief, he called the attention of his commanding officer to the wound, and the officer ordered him to the rear. Campbell went in search of his regiment's surgeon. Amid "great confusion" he found retreating troops, ambulances, horses, and wounded soldiers. Refused admittance to any of the already full wagons that could carry him from the battlefield, Campbell cut loose an old, lame horse from a wagon but quickly realized that the beast would not be reliable if he was forced to flee the battlefield. Spotting some State Guard cavalry horses tied nearby, Campbell appropriated two. When he found other wounded men from his regiment, he left one horse for them and set out on the other horse to find help.[8]

Joseph Martin of Company K, First Kansas, found that a friend had been wounded in the thigh with two bullets. He had promised the man's mother that he would take care of him if any "accident" happened, so Martin carried his wounded friend to the rear. He dressed his wound and placed him in a hospital wagon to be carried to town. "Many of the wagons were heaping full," he wrote, but the friend "depended on me to take care of him which I did."[9] Bacon, Campbell, and Martin's friend were lucky—they survived their wounds when so many wounded perished from lack of medical attention, or later from infection.

Despite the Southern pressure, the thirty-five hundred men and ten guns of the formidable Federal battle line on Bloody Hill held firm. Their elevated position on the plateau gave them an advantage, but the Federals were also able to stand fast because of the uncoordinated nature of the enemy attacks. The uneven terrain, prairie grass, and brush, the inexperience of the men, and their lack of ammunition played havoc with Southern attempts to concentrate their superior numbers and firepower against Bloody Hill. Although the entire State Guard line may have started the assault in unison, when they came under fire, units reacted differently. Portions of the line went to ground and stayed put, other commands continued to advance, and still others retreated. Men carefully husbanded ammunition to make every shot count. Nevertheless, as Maj. John M. Schofield of Brigadier General Lyon's staff reported, "The battle raged with unabated fury for more than an hour, the scale seeming all the time nearly equally balanced, our troops sometimes gaining a little ground and again giving way a few yards to rally again."[10]

The most intense fighting took place around the Federal artillery batteries, commanded by Capt. James Totten and Lt. John DuBois. From these skillfully manned strong points in the Federal line came devastating rounds of canister that thinned the Southern ranks and helped force back the assaults. State Guardsman Bacon developed a healthy respect for the Federal

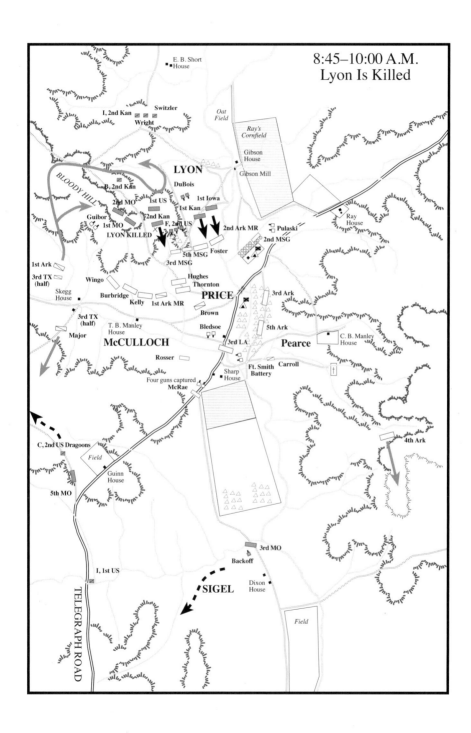

8:45–10:00 A.M.
Lyon Is Killed

artillery. "No human courage can be of any avail against such machinery," he explained, as men massed against cannon are like men against a steam engine.[11] The capture of even one of the batteries probably would have forced the collapse of the Union line of battle, a fact that Maj. Gen. Sterling Price himself recognized. After the battle, Price told a Springfield secessionist that he would "gladly have given his life" to have taken Totten's Battery, and indeed had tried to do so.[12] At several times during the fighting, the Southerners reached within thirty or forty yards of the Federal artillery pieces. "To silence or capture our batteries occupied their thoughts," wrote US regular John Dailey. "They looked upon them as our main reliance, and when they were gone everything else, they supposed, would go to pieces."[13]

Artillery fire from batteries on both sides was devastatingly effective during the fight for Bloody Hill. Although most infantrymen carried a limited amount of small-arms cartridges, artillery batteries in both armies were apparently well supplied with ammunition and kept up a steady rate of fire. Missouri State Guard doctor John Snyder noticed a Federal sharpshooter hiding behind a large hollow tree who would step out to take shots at the Guardsmen. Snyder pointed out the marksman to General Parsons, who ordered one of the pieces of Capt. Henry Guibor's battery to take a shot. A six-pounder was carefully sighted, and when the Federal soldier popped out, fired, and went behind the tree, the artillery piece barked. No more was heard of the sharpshooter, and after the battle Parsons and Snyder found that the solid shot had torn and splintered the tree and passed through the sharpshooter, tearing him to pieces.[14]

State Guardsman W. O. Coleman, an officer in Gen. James McBride's division, narrowly escaped death when the "noted race horse" he was riding was struck by canister from Totten's Battery. The iron balls struck the horse from head to tail, and the left stirrup and rein were shot in half. Coleman's men counted sixty-seven holes in the animal.[15] On the opposite side, one Federal solid shot decapitated a State Guard captain, traveled through his lieutenant's body from side to side, and killed two men behind him. One Kansan wrote home that when a load of canister was fired into the enemy, "you ought to have seen the miserable rascals fall. It would open their ranks so quick it would make your head swim."[16] Even if an artillery round missed its target, the effect of the shot could be more than a little unnerving. One soldier wrote of watching the earth part like "some invisible plow was tearing up a great furrow"; then a whistle like a steam engine announced that a solid shot was ricocheting over his head and burying itself behind him.[17]

Acts of personal bravery by company, regimental, and even, division commanders, so common on Civil War battlefields, were clearly in evidence on Bloody Hill. One of the reasons that the inexperienced soldiers on both sides were able to fight so well was because of the inspirational leadership of their officers. Gen. John B. Clark of the State Guard was severely wounded in the leg, but said it was "nothing." When finally faint from loss of blood, Clark agreed to go to the rear but told his men, "I know you will do your duty." Col. John Q. Burbridge of the State Guard was hit in the head, but as he was carried away, he shouted, "Missourians, never run!" to his men and ordered an officer to "lead the men nearer the enemy, and pay no regard to me." A Lt. C. Kent of the State Guard, wounded slightly three times, paid the wounds no attention and was finally carried to the rear when a bullet penetrated his lungs.[18] Col. Richard H. Weightman, a Mexican War veteran and commander of a brigade in the State Guard's Eighth Division, recklessly exposed himself to enemy fire in advance of his men until he fell wounded in three places.[19] "All our field officers were mounted and close up behind us," remembered State Guardsman Bacon. "I could see how we might escape casualty, but I could not see how these officers could avoid stopping some of the missiles that flew so thickly overhead."[20]

Their Federal counterparts were just as steady. Lt. Col. William H. Merritt of the First Iowa, wearing a white coat and riding a white horse, rode up and down the line, presenting a clear target, "as cool and imperturbable as though it were raindrops, instead of bullets, which were pelting every object around him. His manner and voice inspired his men with confidence, and kept them steady under that appalling fire," one of his men wrote.[21] Capt. Alexander L. Mason of the First Iowa "was ever at his post, laboring for the general welfare of his men, and for their proficiency in drill and manual of arms." Thinking that a musket was more serviceable than a sword, Mason was loading his weapon when he was wounded in the leg and died about a half hour later. His last words were, "Throw no time away on me; move on, boys, and give them your best."[22] Lt. Rinaldo A. Barker of Company K, First Kansas, was wounded in three places. With his face and body covered with blood, he waved his sword and refused to leave the field. Finally, he yelled, "Boys, go into them!" and joined his men in a charge.[23]

Such bravado characterized the army's commanders as well, in one case with fatal results. Brig. Gen. Ben McCulloch personally led his Louisianans against Colonel Sigel, whereas Major General Price and Brigadier General Lyon remained dangerously close to the front line on Bloody Hill to inspire their men and direct their movements. Price took a minor wound in the side, and Lyon was wounded in the leg and head. Lyon was a relatively new general (as, indeed, they all were), but unlike McCulloch and Price, he had spent his entire adult life in the military, and nearly all his career as a junior officer. He felt at ease personally leading men into combat. During the desperate fighting on Bloody Hill, Lyon must have mentally reverted back to his days as a company commander rather than thinking as a commanding general.

About 9:30 a.m., the confusion of battle created a gap in the Federal line. Lyon ordered Col. Robert B. Mitchell's Second Kansas into the gap and then rode beside Mitchell as his unit marched in that direction, no doubt to show Mitchell where to place his regiment. But the Federals were, in the words of one Kansan, "unaware of the close proximity of the enemy." As Lyon turned to his right to watch the Kansans wheel into line, disaster struck. "All at once from the trees and bushes came a murderous volley, the head of the column being but a few yards from the ambushed [sic] rebels. Gen. Lyon and Col. Mitchell being on horseback were conspicuous marks."[24] Shots tore into the mounted officers and the leading companies of the

John B. Clark, Jr., was a major in the First Infantry Regiment, Third Division, Missouri State Guard.

Second Kansas. A rifle bullet entered Lyon's left side, plowed through his heart and both lungs, and exited the opposite side. The Federal commander was dead almost immediately.

Lyon's death would inspire many poets and artists, each with a slightly different version of the general's last moments, and rouse a fierce debate among veterans for decades after the battle. Even among eyewitnesses there was little agreement about exactly what happened when Lyon and the Kansans received the "death volley." The most oft-quoted account has Lyon waving his hat and shouting, "Come on, my brave boys, I will lead you forward!"[25] But how did Lyon actually behave? One eyewitness, Alexander Becher, a private in Company K of the Second Kansas, wrote years after the war that he did not recall Lyon swinging his hat or yelling anything inspiring. Instead, Becher remembered Lyon "very distinctly and emphatically" giving the necessary commands to move the Kansans into position. In another disputed detail, some writers have claimed that Lyon fell into the arms of a nearby officer or even his orderly, but Becher recalled that the general simply leaned on Maj. William Cloud of the Second Kansas for a few moments and then expired. An officer remembered Lyon's orderly gently lowering the general to the ground. A detail of men from the Second Kansas then bore his body to the rear.[26]

The same State Guard volley that killed Lyon struck Mitchell. Hit just below the knee ("a pretty severe flesh wound"), Mitchell remained in the saddle. A few minutes later, he suffered a second and far more serious wound when a ball entered his left thigh just above the groin and passed through his body, fortunately without fracturing any bones. Some time later, weak from loss of blood, Mitchell moved about three hundred yards to his right and was about to dismount under a tree. Unknown to him, two State Guardsmen were approaching to try to take him prisoner. At the last moment, when they were upon him, Mitchell shot one dead with his revolver. When he tried to shoot the other, the percussion cap snapped without setting off the charge. Mitchell then drew his sword and struck the second man on the head with the back of it, knocking him senseless. Mitchell escaped to his own lines and turned command of the regiment over to Charles Blair, his lieutenant colonel.[27] In Blair's words, "Colonel Mitchell sent for me and ordered me to take charge of the battalion, and see that it maintained the reputation of Kansas."[28]

With Lyon dead, the Federals continued to cling grimly to Bloody Hill as Maj. Samuel Sturgis, the highest-ranking regular army officer not dead or wounded, assumed command. With ammunition running low and casualties mounting, the Southerners gambled on a change in tactics. With the attention of the Federals fixed on the infantry assault, the Southerners planned a simultaneous cavalry attack to outflank the Union line. In response to a plea for help from Major

General Price, Brigadier General McCulloch ordered Col.
Elkanah Greer and his Texans to take that assignment. Greer's
men had been scattered from the Sharp farm by Colonel Sigel's
brigade, so now the Texan had only about half his regiment in
hand, or about 400 men. Greer moved his men west along
Skegg's Branch (an east-west tributary of Wilson's Creek, on
the southern edge of Bloody Hill) and then north through a
ravine that brought them undetected into position only about
three or four hundred yards from the Union right flank. On the
way, Greer picked up Col. DeRosey Carroll's First Arkansas
Cavalry—an additional 350 men.

Greer impetuously ordered his men to charge, but a number
of factors worked against a successful attack. Thick undergrowth
and the uncoordinated efforts of both officers and men to get raw,
undisciplined troops into position produced disorder. Not everyone heard the order to charge, so only three companies, or about
240 men, actually came crashing down on the Federals, with
Greer leading the charge "in a dashing and gallant manner."[29] It
was "possibly the most thrilling moment of [my] life," wrote a
State Guardsmen who was cheering Greer's troopers.

The startled Union infantrymen quickly sized up the situation and fell back, under the guns of Captain Totten and
Lieutenant DuBois, and calmly waited for the Texans. At a
range of about forty paces, half of the Federals in the area
fired, and as the Texans veered away, the other half blazed
away. Soon clouds of dust and smoke enveloped both sides, so
that only the red gleam of cannon fire and the flash of muskets
and pistols could be seen, with an occasional riderless horse
emerging from the cloud. The "wild and wonderful" charge
was soon turned back, and order was restored in the Federal
ranks.[30] The action was brief, but so intense that a Federal
artilleryman was able to recall the Texans being close enough
to distinctly hear the crushing of bones of men and horses.[31]
At approximately 10:00 a.m., with part of the Federals' attention temporarily diverted to driving off Colonel Greer, Major

Col. Robert Byington Mitchell led the Second Kansas Infantry at Wilson's Creek.

General Price ordered his men to break off the fight and retreat down Bloody Hill. The second Southern assault had ended, but the battle was far from over.

The four-and-a-half-hour fight for Bloody Hill had devastated the bucolic Missouri landscape. A Kansas soldier described the ugly scene that surrounded both sides: "The dead . . . all bloody and ghastly, presented a pitiable sight; the wounded crying out with pain, or beseeching for water, well nigh unnerved the stoutest heart. Guns, accoutrements, and all the paraphernalia of war were scattered about in every direction."[32]

Having survived another Southern drive, Major Sturgis held a quick council of war with his officers. "In this perplexing condition of affairs," Sturgis wrote, the question posed by most of his officers was "Is retreat possible?" The council was brought to a close by the advance of a large column of infantry from the opposite side of Wilson's Creek, where Sigel had started his bombardment that morning. "Supposing they were Sigel's men," Sturgis reported, "the line was formed for an advance, with the hope of forming a junction with him."[33]

But Sturgis was about to realize what Colonel Sigel had discovered so painfully earlier that morning. The advancing "friendly" troops were in fact the enemy. Brigadier General McCulloch and Major General Price were not finished with the Federals. They were returning again—this time, with more men.

17

THE FINAL ATTACK AND THE END OF THE BATTLE

After two failed attempts, Maj. Gen. Sterling Price tried once more to capture Bloody Hill. For the third attack, he called on Brig. Gens. Ben McCulloch and Nicholas B. Pearce to bolster his State Guard and bring overwhelming numbers to bear on Maj. Samuel Sturgis and the Federals. McCulloch contributed the remainder of the Third Louisiana, and Pearce brought his entire Third Arkansas, most of his Fifth Arkansas, and the Fort Smith Battery to Bloody Hill.

About 10:30 a.m., three thousand Southerners moved up the hill, and as Union staff officer Maj. John Schofield wrote, "The fiercest and most bloody engagement of the day" began, "and the smoke of the opposing lines was often so confounded as to seem but one. Now for the first time during the day our entire line maintained its position with perfect firmness. Not the slightest disposition to give way was manifested at any

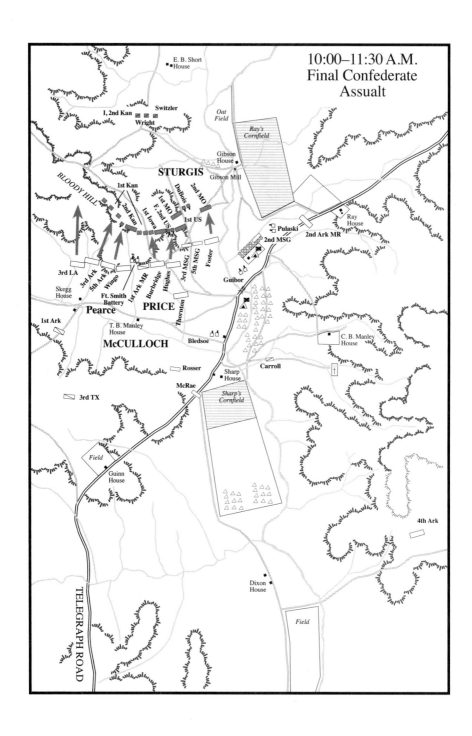

10:00–11:30 A.M.
Final Confederate
Assualt

point, till finally the enemy gave way and fled from the field."[1] William Wherry, one of Brig. Gen. Nathaniel Lyon's aides, noticed the "unabated ardor and impetuosity" of the enemy. "The flash and roar were incessant, and the determined Southrons repeatedly advanced nearly to the muzzles of the pieces of their foes, only to be hurled back before the withering fire as from the blast of a furnace."[2]

Pearce recalled that "volley after volley was poured against our lines, and our gallant boys were cut down like grass," but the survivors would "win or die."[3] Col. John Gratiot of the Third Arkansas

William M. Wherry, General Lyon's aide-de-camp and a first lieutenant, received the Medal of Honor for distinguished gallantry at Wilson's Creek.

wrote of "one of the most terrific fires ever endured by men, so heavy that the whole regiment had to lay down, and fire in that position." They "stood to it like men," reported Gratiot, and "poured in vol[l]ey after vol[l]ey."[4] Unfortunately, some of Gratiot's men also fell to "friendly fire," when units posted behind them and lower down Bloody Hill shot through their ranks. A member of the First Kansas wrote that the last assault "was the most deadly," and "along our line was one living sheet of fire."[5]

Once again, Federal artillery was decisive. "The enemy could frequently be seen within 20 or 30 feet of his [Totten's] guns," Major Schofield observed.[6] A member of the First Kansas praised a section of Totten's Battery (two guns) that had been detached to support the Union right flank. These pieces did "fearful execution," he wrote, and in fact "saved us from total destruction," with the enemy "nearly cut to pieces."[7] Supporting the guns were the muskets of a depleted by still resolute Union army. Taking advantage of what little natural cover remained—the prairie grass had been trampled earlier that morning—Lt. Col. Charles Blair of the Second Kansas ordered his men to lie down, and when the enemy approached within about fifty yards, he cried, "Now, boys, give 'em h—ll!" and his men sent a crashing volley into the enemy's ranks.[8] The combined Southern forces stood fast, blazing away in return and doing incredible damage as well. A Kansas officer wrote poetically that his men fell around him "like the leaves of the forest in autumn," holding their fire until the enemy came so close "we could see them wink" and then falling "like grass before the scythe" amid "a perfect storm of iron and lead."[9]

After about forty-five minutes, the Southern commanders ordered their men once more to break off contact and re-form at the base of Bloody Hill. Little did they know that they were about to drive the Federals from Bloody Hill after all. Although the third assault had been repulsed, Sturgis was told that the Second Kansas was nearly out of ammunition. With his men exhausted and low on ammunition, large numbers of killed, wounded, and missing, and no word from Col. Franz Sigel, Major Sturgis decided that it was time to retreat. The fiery captain Thomas Sweeny begged Sturgis to reconsider, arguing that they should stay—the Federals had plenty of ammunition scrounged from the cartridge boxes of the dead and wounded, and it was actually the enemy who was retreating and out of ammunition. Capt. Gordon Granger agreed with Sweeny, but Sturgis believed that the enemy still had not brought their reserves into action and that retreat was the only safe option. "We threw away one of the most splendid victories ever achieved on this continent," Sweeny said.[10]

The challenge for Sturgis was to pull his men off Bloody Hill without being overwhelmed in the process. About 11:30

a.m., he ordered his troops to end the battle and save the remnants of the army. After driving off two probing attempts by the Southerners, the Federals withdrew from Bloody Hill and began the retreat back to Springfield. Unlike Sigel's departure, the Federals with Sturgis withdrew in an orderly fashion—a point made by Colonel Blair, who wrote, "My command came off in good order and slow time, with the men as perfectly dressed as on the drill ground."[11] Like Sweeny, some of the Federal enlisted men could not believe they were permanently leaving the field. Some thought they were merely retiring to eat and then would return to the fight. "That we were whipped, and on a retreat, never entered my mind for a moment, "wrote one Kansan.[12]

About two miles from the battlefield, the Federals halted at a spring. Soon one of Sigel's men reached Sturgis and reported that his brigade had been routed, with Sigel himself "either killed or taken prisoner." The retreating column soon met a large part of Sigel's brigade (those units that had escaped intact from the field), and together the regiments marched on to Springfield.[13] Although every man in the Federal ranks was hungry and tired, the retreat was particularly difficult for the wounded. "It was painful to see men wounded in all forms dragging their slow steps along," wrote First Sgt. Hugh Campbell, himself wounded on Bloody Hill, "unable to procure room in the crowded wagons." Campbell found a comrade wounded in the thigh, being supported by two others. Desperate to help his friend, and unable to find room for him in one of the wagons or get a horse for him to ride, the frustrated Campbell asked an officer's African American slave to let the man ride a short distance. When the rider refused, explaining that the horse belonged to an officer, Campbell seized the reins and told the rider that he would shoot him if he did not dismount. The servant did as he was told, and Campbell had the satisfaction of seeing his friend safely to Springfield.[14]

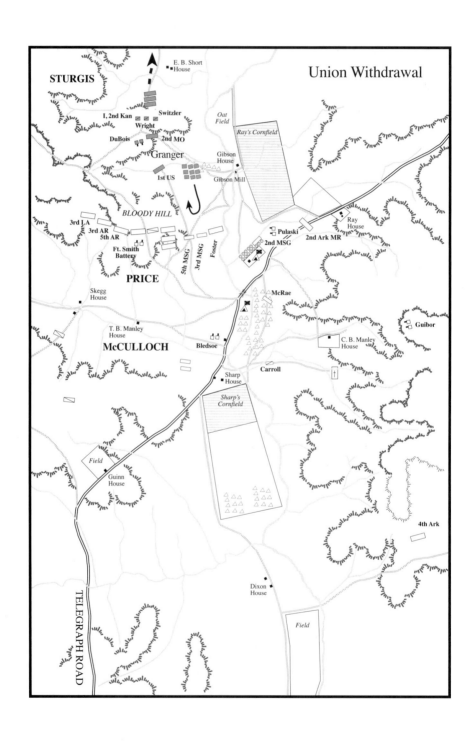

STURGIS

E. B. Short House

Union Withdrawal

Oat Field

Switzler

I, 2nd Kan

Wright

DuBois

2nd MO

Granger

Ray's Cornfield

Gibson House

1st US

Gibson Mill

BLOODY HILL

3rd LA

3rd AR

5th AR

Ft. Smith Battery

5th MSG

3rd MSG

Foster

Pulaski

2nd MSG

2nd Ark MR

Ray House

PRICE

Skegg House

McRae

Guibor

T. B. Manley House

McCULLOCH

Bledsoe

Carroll

C. B. Manley House

Sharp House

Sharp's Cornfield

Field

Guinn House

4th Ark

Dixon House

Field

TELEGRAPH ROAD

Not all the wounded were carried with the army. Some were abandoned on the field. Robert Friedrich of the Second Kansas found a good friend in "intense pain" from a bullet that had entered his breast and exited between his shoulder blades. Friedrich took his hat, filled it with leaves, and gave it to his friend for a pillow; then he gave him some water, sat down beside him, and tried to cheer him. Friedrich stayed until the rest of the army had left the field and then "sadly took his hand and bade him good-by. I never saw him again."[15]

The exhausted Southerners cautiously moved up Bloody Hill for a fourth time, only to see the Federals retreating to the north. "A mighty shout of exultation" arose from the Southern ranks, one State Guardsman said.[16] Pursuit, however, was not an option—casualties were heavy in the Southern ranks as well; the men were tired and low on ammunition, units were disorganized, and hundreds of wounded needed treatment.

Major General Price retired to his tent, where Dr. John Snyder found him sitting in the shade, his shirt collar open, in an "unusual good humor." His wound was still bleeding a little, but he was "all right and ready to go right on to Springfield." Snyder exchanged a handshake and congratulations with the general. After being treated to a toddy from Price's liquor chest, Snyder, like all the survivors along Wilson's Creek, "felt triumphant over the combined tyrannies of heat, hunger and the Lincoln administration."[17]

So closed "one of the most bloody and obstinately fought battles of the war, and for inexperienced troops the most remarkable in the obstinate persistency with which the fight was maintained," wrote Major Schofield.[18]

Now Major Sturgis and Brigadier General McCulloch faced difficult decisions. With the bloody fight over, would the Federals continue their retreat through Missouri? And would the Southerners be able to capitalize on their victory?

18

"A Savage and Desperate Courage"

At 5:00 p.m., the battered and physically spent Federals threw themselves down to rest in the streets of Springfield and began to discuss their fate.

"You never saw such hard looking fellows," wrote one Kansan. "The powder so completely blackened their faces that you could hardly tell one from the other."[1] Many had bruised shoulders from the "vigorous thumping" of muskets that had slammed into them each time they pulled the trigger on Bloody Hill.[2]

Those wounded who had been successfully evacuated from the battlefield began their long wait for treatment. Newspaper correspondent Franc Wilkie found the military hospital in town was soon full, and with it the Bailey House Hotel and the Methodist church. Ghastly sights awaited those who visited any of the medical facilities: "Some of the wounds were horrible—some had the lower jaw shot away, others had arms torn

Drawing of Springfield done in the fall of 1861 by Wilson's Creek veteran Andrew Tinkham.

off, others came in with legs dangling over the sides of the wagon—all thirsty, and calling almost incessantly for water."[3]

Although some Federal units had survived the battle virtually unscathed, others had suffered devastating losses. The First Kansas and First Missouri, regiments that had borne the brunt of the fighting on Bloody Hill, had lost respectively 106 and 103 killed in action or mortally wounded. These units earned the dubious honor of being among the Union infantry regiments with the greatest number of killed in a single engagement in the entire war. Company C of the First Iowa, the regiment's color company, entered the fight with 79 officers and men. After the company's captain was mortally wounded and the first lieutenant seriously wounded, a private ("an experienced and tried soldier") took command. By the end of the fighting, the unit had lost 3 dead, 21 seriously wounded, and 6 slightly wounded—a total of 30 men, or nearly 40 percent of the company.[4] Company G of the First Kansas took 93 men into the fight and had 55 left unscathed by day's end. A total of 1,317 Federals, or nearly a quarter of the strength of the Army of the West, were casualties at Wilson's Creek.[5]

But the Union commanders faced a much more pressing problem than treating their wounded and counting their losses. A battered but intact Southern army was still only ten miles away, and, if the Federals remained, they would soon be facing another tough fight, this time from house to house in Springfield.

That evening, Maj. Samuel Sturgis called a council of war. All the officers present agreed that retreat to Rolla was the only option. Although precisely what happened at the council is unknown, Sturgis yielded command of the army to Col. Franz Sigel, incorrectly assuming with everyone else that Sigel had received his commission as brigadier general and was now the senior officer. Sigel no doubt encouraged such a belief. He issued orders for the army to march at two o'clock the following morning.[6]

Not everyone agreed with the retreat order. Capt. Thomas Sweeny had persuaded Brig. Gen. Nathaniel Lyon to hold Springfield and fight and had tried to dissuade Sturgis from leaving the battlefield, so his reaction to the retreat order was predictable. Sweeny had been wounded twice during the battle and was being treated by Dr. E. C. Franklin when the council of war was held. When told that the Federals would abandon the town, Sweeny with "an oath . . . exclaimed, 'The enemy were retreating, why in h—ll should we run too,' or words to this effect."[7]

Despite his orders, Sigel was still asleep at 2:00 a.m. The army finally began leaving town at four o'clock, and the rear guard did not clear Springfield until about 6:00 a.m. Accompanied by a large number of Unionist refugees, the command was strung out along the road to Rolla, halting for long periods. But it traveled about twenty miles the first day. The haggard rear guard was in the saddle from 2:00 a.m. to 11:00 p.m. On the second day, the Federals only made seven miles, the officers supposing that Sigel was attempting another "Carthage tactic" to lure the enemy into attacking him. On the third day, the army covered twenty-three miles, bringing it to the town of Lebanon on the afternoon of August 13.

At Lebanon, another council of war was held, with disastrous results for Colonel Sigel. Many of his officers were at the point of revolt, clamoring for the return of Major Sturgis to command. They argued that if indeed Sigel was trying to duplicate his success at Carthage, the weakened army could not afford to fight another battle. They complained that the volunteers were receiving preferential treatment over the regulars, as the professional soldiers had been constantly assigned duty as the rear guard, five miles from the vanguard of the column, and did not reach camp until midnight. Finally, the officers cited depredations committed by straggling troops and asserted that "a general spirit of insubordination" had taken hold of the men. Even more damning, when an incorrect rumor was received that Confederate forces from southeast Missouri were coming to cut off and overwhelm the column, Sigel advocated destroying the Federal artillery and wagons and making a forced march to Rolla.

Finally prodded into action, Sturgis questioned Sigel whether he had in fact received his general's commission. When Sigel confessed that he had not, Sturgis informed the colonel, over his protests, that he would take command of the army once again. Sturgis started the column for Rolla, and harmony was restored. From that point, the Federals made steady progress and arrived in Rolla on August 17. There Sigel learned that he had, in fact, been commissioned a brigadier general of volunteers.[8]

Back in Springfield, the first Southern troops entered the city not long after the Federal troops departed. A Confederate flag presented to a company of the Third Texas Cavalry by the women of Henderson was unfurled from the top of the Greene County Courthouse, and "as it was lifted in the breeze, a shout went up which made the very heavens ring."[9] The victorious brigadier general Ben McCulloch issued a proclamation to the area's civilians and general orders to his troops. His message to the civilian population spoke of his "great and signal victory" but also reassured them that the rights and property of all, including Union sympathizers, would be protected. McCulloch told his men how proud he was of their performance. "Nobly have you sustained yourselves," he wrote, and thanks to "great gallantry and determined courage," they had routed the enemy "with great slaughter." "Your first battle has been glorious," he said, and now the flag of the Confederacy floated over the "stronghold of the enemy."[10]

But McCulloch and his men faced serious problems despite their victory. Southern losses had been heavy. At least 12 percent of the Western Army was dead, wounded, or missing— some 1,222 men.[11] Some units had been hit hard. Joseph Mudd reported that of the seven captains in his State Guard regiment, two had been killed and a third was severely wounded. The regiment had taken somewhere between 200 and 270 men into action, and at least 104 were dead or wounded—probably more.[12] Col. Thomas Churchill's First Arkansas Mounted Rifles had entered the fight with about 600 men. By the end of the battle, nearly a third were casualties.

Equally troubling, as Lyon had discovered, keeping a large number of well troops, let alone hundreds of wounded, supplied in Springfield was problematic at best. The Southern wounded were soon transferred from the battlefield into town and had to share their accommodations with those badly wounded Federals who had been left behind when Sturgis retreated to Rolla. Southern surgeons and attendants were hard-pressed to give the wounded even basic services. A week after the battle, Dr. W. A. Cantrell of Arkansas wrote that from the time the battle

opened to that moment, "I have seen and heard nothing but gun-
shot wounds and the groans of the dying and distressed." Many
of the wounded were receiving poor medical attention and "the
greater portion no attention at all," Cantrell complained—"a
hundred doctors could be employed constantly."[13]

In the wake of the battle, soldiers and civilians on both
sides tried to sort out exactly what had happened along the
banks of Wilson's Creek. It is clear from a careful reading
of battle accounts that, with some exceptions, the majority
of soldiers on both sides fought particularly well, given their
inexperience. What one State Guardsman wrote could apply to
nearly all the battle's participants: the men performed "their
bloody work with the coolness and method of the farmer or
mechanic at his daily task."[14] A Kansan agreed, writing that
the battle gave "considerable glory per capita."[15] Most Union
and Southern soldiers had maintained their personal honor
by bravely doing their duty in the fight, with some perform-
ing particularly heroic actions. But most soldiers also maintained their "corporate honor" on the battlefield, not disgrac-
ing their state or town through cowardly actions, honoring
the vitally important unwritten social contract that existed
between the volunteers and the citizens of their states and
local communities.

Who actually won the fight was much harder for veterans
to sort out. Men on both sides claimed victory. To Union veterans, they had accomplished what they had set out to do:
stun the enemy and retreat in safety. To their way of thinking,
they had at least fought the enemy to a draw, if they did not
score an outright victory. Kansan H. S. Moore was typical. He
believed that "it was a great battle, and a glorious Union victory."[16] Another Union soldier derisively noted that if indeed it
was a Confederate victory, it was at best a Pyrrhic one, with
many more such triumphs sure to destroy the Confederate
army: "Let the South call this a victory or what they please,"
he chided.[17]

Southern veterans saw Wilson's Creek as their decisive victory. They had been surprised, it is true, but they had rallied, fought hard, and forced Brigadier General Lyon's army to withdraw, leaving them in possession of the field, and therefore the victors. Some argued that neither side had scored a clear-cut victory: "The battle ended in a fair draw, and undecided as to which had been worsted," wrote one participant.[18]

The one thing veterans on both sides could agree on was that Wilson's Creek was a desperate struggle, a rough introduction to soldiering, and a tribute to the fighting qualities of the ordinary soldier. A State Guardsman characterized the battle as "no more nor less than a rough-and-tumble fight, and there is not much credit due except to the private soldier."[19] Many soldiers were shocked by the brutal nature of the fighting. A Kansas veteran wrote a few days after the battle, "I never thought men could be so cruel to one another. . . . I heard men say it was the hardest fight we have had in this country, and they were men that knew. For my part, I don't want more like it while I am in the service of Uncle Sam."[20] Lt. Newell Spicer recalled, "Both sides seemed determined not to leave the field so long as a man was left, so they fought on with a savage and desperate courage which has scarcely a parallel in the annals of civilized warfare."[21] Another veteran was disturbed by how the battle had transformed him: "When I see one of them [the enemy] fall I cry out 'good,' and laugh. Never did I think a man could get his heart so cold as we did on that occasion."[22]

Tragically, many veterans of Wilson's Creek honed their killing skills on far bloodier fields of battle, from Pea Ridge to Chickamauga to the battles around Vicksburg and Atlanta. As one editorial writer explained many years after the battle, "To the great mass of the men engaged it was a first fight, but there was no panic, no stampede, nothing to apologize for at Wilson's Creek. It was one of the most savage and stubborn conflicts of a war marked by many such. . . . The 10th of August is a notable day in the history of our country."[23]

Stone cairn marking the traditional site of Brig. Gen. Nathaniel Lyon's death, circa 1897.

Within a few days of the end of the battle, when the Southerners established camps around Springfield, the three generals held their own council of war. Maj. Gen. Sterling Price wanted to follow up their victory and pressed Brigadier General McCulloch to march with him to the Missouri River. There he could get recruits from north of the river and disrupt Union control of the Missouri. But McCulloch disagreed, explaining that his troops were low on ammunition, his

men were needed to pro-
tect northern Arkansas
and the Indian Territory
from Federal invasion, and
they could expect no help
from Confederate forces in
southeast Missouri. Brig.
Gen. Nicholas Pearce's
Arkansas State troops
were finished with this
campaign and ready to
march back home to be discharged. As an alternative,
McCulloch suggested that
Price fortify Springfield,
have the Missouri legislature gather there, vote the
state out of the Union, and
accept the State Guard into

Maj. Peter J. Osterhaus of the Second Missouri Infantry (US) survived the Battle of Wilson's Creek and commanded a division at Pea Ridge.

Confederate service. When an overall theater commander was named, he reasoned, they could march to the river, the Missourians could get their recruits, and the Confederates could move against Saint Louis.[24]

The Missouri general was not interested in such plans. He would follow his own course. In preparation for his move north, he reassumed overall command of the Missouri State Guard, and the fragile Southern coalition formed the month before passed into history. On August 25, his State Guardsmen left Springfield, bound for the river county of Lafayette and the town of Lexington. Price surrounded a Federal force of thirty-five hundred Illinois and Missouri troops there, and after a three-day siege (September 18–20), the Federals surrendered. Price had scored his second dramatic victory in six weeks and gained thousands of recruits for the State Guard.

But his success was temporary. Finally prodded into action by Brigadier General Lyon's death and the twin defeats of Wilson's Creek and Lexington, Western Department commander Maj. Gen. John C. Fremont left Saint Louis with thirty-eight thousand men to destroy the State Guard and secure Missouri for a Federal advance down the Mississippi. Price wisely told many of his recruits to return to their homes and retreated from Lexington to avoid being trapped by Fremont. He moved into extreme southwest Missouri, beyond Fremont's immediate reach. On October 25, an advance party of the slow-moving Union army recaptured Springfield, and soon the rest of the Federal army settled into town. The stage was set for another decisive battle in southwest Missouri.

Unfortunately for "the Pathfinder," Abraham Lincoln had had enough of Fremont. Smarting over a proclamation he had issued prematurely freeing the slaves of those Missourians in rebellion, and disappointed with his slow pursuit of Price, President Lincoln officially relieved Fremont of command on November 2 and replaced him with Gen. David Hunter. Fremont's army, like Lyon's, was far from its base of supplies, unable to deal a crippling blow to an elusive enemy, and facing the approaching winter. Hunter, "in conformity with the views of the President," abandoned Springfield and dispersed his army. In the wake of the Federal withdrawal, Price advanced north to the town of Osceola, where he remained about three weeks. By Christmas 1861, he had reoccupied Springfield and made the city his winter quarters.

In February 1862, a new Union force of some twelve thousand men, including some Wilson's Creek veterans, marched southwest from Rolla in a difficult and daring winter campaign. Brig. Gen. Samuel Curtis drove Price and his mixed force of eight thousand Confederates and State Guardsmen from Springfield and into northwest Arkansas. While Curtis adopted a defensive stance near Bentonville, Price joined forces with

Brigadier General McCulloch again, but this time McCulloch would not be in overall command of a coalition army. The new Confederate commander, Maj. Gen. Earl Van Dorn, launched his own bold offensive against Curtis. In two days of savage fighting northeast of Bentonville, near the local landmark of Elkhorn Tavern and the land mass known as Pea Ridge, Van Dorn was decisively defeated and McCulloch was killed. Although the Confederates were able to launch cavalry raids into Missouri after Pea Ridge, the battle ended any serious Confederate attempt to retake the state. For the secession-ists of Missouri, the victories at Wilson's Creek and Lexington represented a high-water mark, the last reasonable hope that Price and his supporters would have to seriously threaten Union control of Missouri.

That is not to say that Confederate sympathizers passively accepted Federal dominance of Missouri after Pea Ridge. In 1863, Confederate commanders Joseph Shelby and General John Marmaduke launched sizable cavalry raids into the state to recruit, capture supplies, confuse the enemy, and draw Union forces away from other threatened parts of the Confederacy. In the fall of 1864, Major General Price himself led the greatest Confederate cavalry foray into Missouri. He failed to destroy the Union garrison at Pilot Knob, threatened but did not capture either Saint Louis or Jefferson City, and was finally beaten at Westport and forced to retreat through Kansas, Missouri, and Arkansas.

Apart from these organized raids, numerous small bands of Confederate partisans raised havoc with Union soldiers and civilians. Federal volunteers and state militia troops brutalized the guerrillas and their supporters in kind, creating a vicious and bloody cycle of revenge and retaliation that sometimes made the bloodletting at Wilson's Creek seem tame by com-parison. In the words of Lyon biographer Christopher Phillips, "The truest meaning of the term civil war was nowhere more apparent than in Missouri."[25]

Nearly 150 years after Wilson's Creek, students of the Civil War, particularly those west of the Mississippi River, still hotly debate the events in Saint Louis and the rest of the Missouri Campaign of 1861. A number of questions immediately come to mind. How important was Wilson's Creek? Did Brigadier General Lyon sacrifice himself in an unnecessary battle? Would Missouri have been plunged into a bitter fratricidal struggle if another commander had led the Union forces? Could Lyon have halted at Boonville and still maintained control of the state? There are no simple answers, and historians must study virtually every action by Lyon, Price, and McCulloch to argue their cases.

Almost everyone agrees on a number of points, however. Wilson's Creek was an important and hard-fought battle, the culmination of a long and difficult campaign. Because the stakes were so high in Missouri, politicians, military leaders, and ordinary soldiers on both sides were under extreme pressure to produce results. Generals grumbled and begged for resources, but given the limited means at their disposal, the major commanders accomplished a great deal—arguably more than in any other theater of war in 1861. The battle was a vital "training ground" for men who would go on to lead troops in some of the most important battles of the war. Wilson's Creek demonstrated that relatively untrained volunteers, when properly led and motivated, could become effective soldiers.

Few doubted that the Battle of Wilson's Creek focused national attention on the war in Missouri and led to greater Federal military activity in the state, directly resulting in the Battle of Pea Ridge, which saved Missouri for the Union. The Southern victory near Springfield was the great "what if" of history, as Price and McCulloch's coalition army failed to follow up their advantage and cause more havoc in Missouri. Although partisans on both sides will forever question the motives of the leaders in Missouri, in the end the only thing that is abundantly clear is that ideologically driven men were convinced that Missouri was too valuable a prize to be lost.

They, in turn, persuaded many citizens that neutrality was not a viable option. All the major players in the Wilson's Creek drama saw that decisive action was required to save their respective causes. Brigadier generals Lyon and McCulloch, Governor Claiborne Fox Jackson, Major General Price, and the thousands of men who bravely fought and died with them must share any blame or credit for what took place in Missouri in the summer of 1861.

NOTES

Introduction

1. Thomas L. Snead, *The Fight for Missouri from the Election of Lincoln to the Death of Lyon* (New York: Charles Scribner's Sons, 1886), 198–200. At least one other version of Brigadier General Lyon's speech exists. "Better, sir, far better, that the blood of every man, woman, and child of the State should flow," Lyon supposedly said, "than that she should successfully defy the Federal Government." James Peckham, *Gen. Nathaniel Lyon, and Missouri in 1861* (New York: American News Co., 1866), 248. Governor Jackson biographer Christopher Phillips believes that the Peckham version is less dramatic but probably more accurate. Christopher Phillips, *Missouri's Confederate: Claiborne Fox Jackson and the Creation of Southern Identity in the Border West* (Columbia: University of Missouri Press, 2000), 257.

Chapter 1

1. The full text of Jackson's inaugural speech may be found in Buel Leopard and Floyd C. Shoemaker, *The Messages and Proclamations of the Governors of the State of Missouri*, 12 vols. (Columbia: The State Historical Society of Missouri, 1922), III: 328–342.
2. Snead, *The Fight for Missouri*, 66.
3. Joseph C. G. Kennedy, *Population of the United States in 1860; Compiled from the Original Returns of the Eighth Census, under the direction of the Secretary of the Interior* (Washington, D.C.: Government Printing Office, 1864), 287, 297–301. According to Kennedy's figures, Missouri in 1860 contained slightly more than one million free whites and African Americans, plus 114,000 slaves. Considering the free population of Missouri as a whole, nearly 100,000 claimed Kentucky as a birthplace, 73,500 were from Tennessee, nearly 54,000 were natives of Virginia, and 475,000 were natives of Missouri. Foreign-born residents of the state numbered 160,000, with natives of the German states accounting for nearly 88,500 of that total. Natives of Ireland made up the second-largest ethnic group in Missouri (nearly 43,500). The city of Saint Louis had 159,000 free persons and 1,500 slaves. Of the free population in Saint Louis County (Kennedy did not report the nativity of Saint Louis city residents), 90,000 were native born, while 96,000 were foreign born.
4. Steven Rowan, ed., *Memoirs of a Nobody: The Missouri Years of an Austrian Radical, 1849–1866* (St. Louis: Missouri Historical Society Press, 1997), 262–263.

Chapter 2

1. Rowan, *Memoirs of a Nobody*, 275.
2. US War Department, *The War of the Rebellion: A Compilation of the Official Records of the Union and Confederate Armies*, 128 vols. (Washington, D.C.: Government Printing Office, 1880–1901), 1: 82–83.
3. Rowan, *Memoirs of a Nobody*, 275, 281.

Chapter 3

1. US War Department, *The War of the Rebellion*, 3: 4.
2. Ibid.
3. Several estimates differ on the total number of militiamen at Camp Jackson. One contemporary historian gave a total of 1,238 officers and men in the camp, presumably on May 6, with no more than 650 rank and file present for the surrender, the rest on leave. Contemporary reports in the Saint Louis press give the figure of 1,150 on May 8 and 9. Captain Lyon reported the capture of 689 officers and men, whereas Brigadier General Frost reported 635 surrendered. (Saint Louis) *Daily Missouri Democrat*, May 8 and 9, 1861; William Hyde and Howard L. Conard, *Encyclopedia of the History of St. Louis* (New York: Southern History Co., 1899), IV: 2432–2433.

4. Rowan, *Memoirs of a Nobody*, 295–296.
5. (Saint Louis) *The Missouri Republican*, March 19, 1887. A US regular recruit likewise believed the rumor that they were to "attack the Secessionists." George Gardner Smith, *Spencer Kellogg Brown: His Life in Kansas and His Death as a Spy, 1842–1863* (New York: D. Appleton and Co., 1903), 198.
6. State of Missouri, *Proceedings of the Missouri State Convention, held at Jefferson City, July, 1861* (Saint Louis: George Knapp and Co., 1861), 116.
7. *Missouri Republican*, March 19, 1887.
8. Smith, *Spencer Kellogg Brown*, 199.
9. (Saint Louis) *The Weekly Missouri Democrat*, May 14, 1861.
10. *National Tribune*, August 8, 1895.
11. *Weekly Missouri Democrat*, May 14, 1861.
12. Smith, *Spencer Kellogg Brown*, 200.
13. *National Tribune*, October 13, 1887; *Missouri Republican*, March 19, 1887.
14. *National Tribune*, August 8, 1895.
15. *Weekly Missouri Democrat*, May 14, 1861.
16. J. Thomas Scharf, *History of St. Louis City and County, from the Earliest Periods to the Present Day*, 2 vols. (Philadelphia: Louis H. Everts and Co., 1883), 2: 495.
17. Scharf, *History of St. Louis*, 497.
18. *National Tribune*, October 13, 1887.
19. Scharf, *History of St. Louis*, 497.
20. Smith, *Spencer Kellogg Brown*, 201.
21. Ibid., 201. Brown believed that men in two different locations opened fire.
22. Otto C. Lademann, *Missouri Republican*, March 19, 1887.
23. Scharf, *History of St. Louis*, 497.
24. *Weekly Missouri Democrat*, May 14, 1861.
25. Ibid.
26. Scharf, *History of St. Louis*, 498.
27. Ibid., 497.

Chapter 4

1. *Sandusky* (Ohio) *Register*, May 18, 1861.
2. Scharf, *History of St. Louis*, 510.
3. US War Department, *The War of the Rebellion*, 53: 490.
4. Unionist Thomas Gantt wrote General Harney on May 14, thanking him for the proclamation's "patriotic tone and tranquillizing assurances." "Reports Made by General William S. Harney During His Command of the United States Forces in the State of Missouri," 37th Congress, First Session, House of Representatives, Executive Document No. 19, 17.
5. US War Department, *The War of the Rebellion*, 3: 369–372.
6. Snead, *The Fight for Missouri*, 181.
7. *Sandusky Register*, May 18, 1861.
8. Smith, *Spencer Kellogg Brown*, 204.
9. Record and Pension Office, US War Department, *Organization and Status of Missouri Troops (Union and Confederate) in Service during the Civil War* (Washington, D.C.: Government Printing Office, 1902), 250–255.
10. W. F. Switzler, *Switzler's Illustrated History of Missouri, from 1541 to 1877* (Saint Louis: C. R. Barns, 1879), 314–318.
11. US War Department, *The War of the Rebellion*, 3: 374–375.
12. Scharf, *History of St. Louis*, 520.
13. (Saint Louis) *Daily Missouri Republican*, June 11, 1861.
14. Proceedings of the Missouri State Convention, 104.
15. US War Department, *The War of the Rebellion*, 3: 376.
16. Donald J. Stanton, Goodwin F. Berquist, and Paul C. Bowers, eds., *The Civil War Reminiscences of General M. Jeff Thompson* (Dayton: Morningside, 1988), 55.
17. Commander Duke believed that Major General Price "surrendered a great advantage" by disbanding his troops under terms of the agreement, "never to be fully recovered," and "immensely increased the subsequent task of assembling an army." Basil W. Duke, *Reminiscences of General Basil W. Duke, C.S.A.* (New York: Doubleday, Page and Co., 1911), 55.

18. *Weekly Missouri Democrat*, June 11, 1861.
19. "Reports Made by General William S. Harney During His Command of the United States Forces in the State of Missouri," 37th Congress, First Session, House of Representatives, Executive Document No. 19, 17, 21–22, 27, 30–31. On June 5, Harney wrote the adjutant general that although the complaints of depredations had received his careful attention, the majority were "without foundation." His confidence in Major General Price's honor and integrity, the purity of his motives, and his loyalty to the government remained unimpaired. Harney claimed to have suffered "unmerited disgrace" when he was relieved a second time.
20. Scharf, *History of St. Louis*, 520.

Chapter 5

1. *Weekly Missouri Democrat*, June 18, 1861.
2. Ibid.
3. *Missouri Republican*, May 14, 1887.
4. Rowan, *Memoirs of a Nobody*, 315.
5. *Weekly Missouri Democrat*, June 18, 1861.
6. *New York Times*, June 17, 1861.
7. *New York Times*, June 16, 1861.
8. *Chariton* (Missouri) *Courier*, August 8, 1924.
9. Rowan, *Memoirs of a Nobody*, 318.
10. *Weekly Missouri Democrat*, June 18, 1861.
11. Thomas W. Knox, *Camp-Fire and Cotton-Field: Southern Adventure in Time of War* (New York: Blelock and Co., 1865), 42.
12. US War Department, *The War of the Rebellion*, 3: 385.
13. *Weekly Missouri Democrat*, June 25, 1861.
14. Thomas L. Snead, "The First Year of the War in Missouri," *Battles and Leaders of the Civil War*, edited by Robert U. Johnson and C. C. Buel, 4 vols. (New York: Century, 1887), I: 267–268.

Chapter 6

1. *Weekly Missouri Democrat*, July 16, 1861.
2. *Weekly Missouri Democrat*, July 9, 1861.
3. Captain Sweeny did send a message to Colonel Sigel on July 1, authorizing the advance to Carthage, and Sigel replied on the morning of July 4 that he would locate Governor Jackson's force. National Archives, M1098, U.S. Army Generals' Reports of Civil War Service, 1864–1887, Vol. 9, Report 31, Roll 5, 507.
4. Snead, *The Fight for Missouri*, 225.
5. William G. Bek, "The Civil War Diary of John T. Buegel, Union Soldier," Part I, *Missouri Historical Review*, vol. 40, no. 3 (April 1946), 311.
6. J. P. Bell, "Price's Missouri Campaign, 1861," *Confederate Veteran*, vol. 22, no. 6 (June 1914), 271.
7. Jeffrey L. Patrick, ed., "Remembering the Missouri Campaign of 1861: The Memoirs of Lt. W. P. Barlow, Guibor's Battery, Missouri State Guard," *Civil War Regiments*, vol. 5, no. 4 (1997), 31–32.
8. *Missouri Republican*, March 26, 1887.
9. Virginia Easley, ed., "Journal of the Civil War in Missouri, 1861: Henry Martyn Cheavens," *Missouri Historical Review*, vol. 56 (October 1961), 19.
10. Bell, "Price's Missouri Campaign, 1861," 318. I owe a special debt to Christy and Kip Lindberg for sharing this and other references from their extensive research on the Missouri State Guard.
11. Ibid., 272.
12. Patrick, "Remembering the Missouri Campaign," 31.
13. Captain Sweeny apparently intended for Colonel Sigel to occupy Carthage itself, "a strong position," but instead he moved ten miles north of town. The Irishman also thought that Sigel had been saved by his artillerymen. National Archives, M1098, U.S. Army Generals' Reports of Civil War Service, 1864–1887, Roll 5, 869–870.

14. *Missouri Republican*, March 26, 1887.
15. *Weekly Missouri Democrat*, July 16, 1861.
16. Franc B. Wilkie, *The Iowa First. Letters from the War* (Dubuque: Herald Book and Job Establishment, 1861), 86.
17. *Daily Missouri Republican*, July 20, 1861.
18. Patrick, "Remembering the Missouri Campaign," 32.
19. *Daily Missouri Republican*, July 20, 1861.
20. Snead, *The Fight for Missouri*, 237.
21. *Daily Missouri Republican*, July 20, 1861.

Chapter 7

1. *Weekly Missouri Democrat*, July 2, 1861.
2. *Muscatine* (Iowa) *Weekly Journal*, July 12, 1861.
3. *Harper's Weekly*, July 27, 1861.
4. Wilkie, *The Iowa First*, 71–72.
5. *Keokuk* (Iowa) *Daily Gate City*, August 14, 1884.
6. Wilkie, *The Iowa First*, 76.
7. *Dubuque* (Iowa) *Weekly Times*, August 8, 1861; *Muscatine Weekly Journal*, August 2, 1861.
8. Return I. Holcombe, *History of Greene County, Missouri* (Saint Louis: Western Historical Co., 1883), 293.
9. Wilkie, *The Iowa First*, 85.
10. US War Department, *The War of the Rebellion*, 3: 394.
11. *Dubuque Weekly Times*, August 8, 1861.
12. Wilkie, *The Iowa First*, 89–92.
13. *Dubuque Weekly Times*, August 8, 1861.
14. Eugene F. Ware, *The Lyon Campaign in Missouri: Being a History of the First Iowa Infantry* (Topeka: Crane and Co., 1907), 252.
15. *Dubuque Weekly Times*, August 8, 1861.
16. *Weekly Missouri Democrat*, July 30, 1861.

Chapter 8

1. Snead, *The Fight for Missouri*, 238.
2. Ibid., 270.
3. Patrick, "Remembering the Missouri Campaign," 33.
4. Joseph A. Mudd, "What I Saw at Wilson's Creek," *Missouri Historical Review* vol. 8 (January 1914), 92.
5. US War Department, *The War of the Rebellion*, 3: 612.
6. When Camp Jackson was abandoned, the troops moved to Camp Stephens, four miles northeast of Bentonville. W. H. Tunnard, *A Southern Record: The History of the Third Regiment of Louisiana Infantry* (Baton Rouge: By the author, 1866), 42–43.
7. US War Department, *The War of the Rebellion*, 3: 607.
8. Ibid., 3: 611.

Chapter 9

1. Tunnard, *A Southern Record*, 44.
2. US War Department, *The War of the Rebellion*, 3: 623. Brigadier General McCulloch was also to have support from other Confederate commanders. Gen. Leonidas Polk in Memphis ordered subordinates Gideon Pillow and William J. Hardee to move into southeast Missouri from Tennessee and Arkansas respectively, unite, and then move either to trap Brigadier General Lyon or capture Saint Louis and move up the Missouri River. In late July and early August, Pillow and Hardee entered Missouri, but neither commander left the southeast part of the state.
3. US War Department, *The War of the Rebellion*, 3: 395–397, 408.
4. *Davenport* (Iowa) *Daily Democrat and News*, August 8, 1861.
5. (Springfield, MO) *Leader-Democrat*, June 29, 1900.

6. *Mohawk Valley Register* (Fort Plain, New York), August 22, 1861.
7. Wilkie, *The Iowa First*, 97.
8. Frank Moore, ed., *The Rebellion Record: A Diary of American Events, with Documents, Narratives, Illustrative Incidents, Poetry, etc.*, 12 vols. (New York: G. P. Putnam, 1861–1868), II: 468.
9. Ware, *The Lyon Campaign in Missouri*, 273.
10. Although this officer's name is consistently misspelled (even in wartime documents), most sources list the correct spelling of Rieff.
11. This account of Dug Springs is based on reports in the Official Records, two accounts by Captain Rieff (one in the *Missouri Republican*, September 25, 1886, the other in E. R. Hutchins, *The War of the 'Sixties*, published in 1912 by the Neale Publishing Co., New York, pages 166–169), and an account by State Guard doctor John Snyder in the *Missouri Republican*, August 14, 1886. Dr. Snyder reported Southern losses as one killed, one dead of sunstroke, and seven wounded.
12. US War Department, *The War of the Rebellion*, 3: 745.
13. Dr. Snyder, a member of the Missouri State Guard, wrote after the war that Brigadier General McCulloch's real difficulty was not a lack of confidence in the Missourians but rather in himself. Snyder believed that McCulloch could have won fame in command of a regiment or two of cavalry, but as an army commander, hampered by regulations and forced to deal with superiors in Richmond, he was "the right man in the wrong place." Snyder argued that McCulloch was "confused and lost" while in overall command of the Western Army, sacrificed his own judgment and common sense, and gave in to the wishes of Colonel McIntosh, his adjutant. Modern historians, such as Thomas Cutrer, McCulloch's biographer, do not support Snyder's attempt at psychological analysis. *Missouri Republican*, August 14, 1886.
14. John Dailey, "In the Ranks under General Lyon in Missouri—1861: The Observations of a Private Soldier," in *Under Both Flags: A Panorama of the Great Civil War, as represented in story, anecdote, adventure, and the romance of reality* (Philadelphia: People's Publishing Co., 1896), 581.
15. No record of the council of war survives, but this account is based on the Committee on the Conduct of the War testimony of Col. Anselm Albert, Maj. Samuel Sturgis, and Capt. Joseph Plummer, and on the recollections of John Dailey, a US regular private who claimed to have consulted the notes of Capt. Gordon Granger of Lyon's staff. *Report of the Joint Committee on the Conduct of the War*, 3 vols. (Washington, D.C.: Government Printing Office, 1863), Part III, 25–26, 228, 264–265.
16. *National Tribune*, August 22, 1895.
17. *Mohawk Valley Register*, August 22, 1861.
18. When Jackson left Missouri after Carthage, Snead became the State Guard's chief of ordnance on July 11 and acting assistant adjutant general on July 16 (both on Price's staff). Richard C. Peterson, James E. McGhee, Kip A. Lindberg, and Keith I. Daleen, *Sterling Price's Lieutenants: A Guide to the Officers and Organization of the Missouri State Guard, 1861–1865* (Independence, MO: Two Trails Publishing, 2007), 33–34, 36.
19. US War Department, *The War of the Rebellion*, 53: 720–721.
20. Samuel B. Barron, *The Lone Star Defenders* (New York: Neale Publishing Co., 1908), 37.
21. William Watson, *Life in the Confederate Army* (New York: Scribner and Welford, 1888), 201.
22. Tunnard, *A Southern Record*, 47.
23. *Missouri Republican*, August 21, 1886.
24. Mudd, "What I Saw at Wilson's Creek," 93.
25. *Missouri Republican*, August 21, 1886.

Chapter 10

1. *Weekly Missouri Democrat*, August 12, 1861.
2. Major General Fremont officially assumed command of the department on July 25. US War Department, *The War of the Rebellion*, 3: 406, 425.
3. *National Tribune*, August 22, 1895.
4. Ware, *The Lyon Campaign in Missouri*, 304.
5. *National Tribune*, August 22, 1895.
6. *Report of the Joint Committee on the Conduct of the War*, 30.

Chapter 11

1. *Missouri Republican*, August 21, 1886.
2. Ibid., October 10, 1885.
3. Watson, *Life in the Confederate Army*, 210.
4. Ibid., 211; "Reminiscences of N. B. Pearce, (Late) Brig. Genl. Commanding 1st Division, Army of Arkansas, C.S.A.," Arkansas History Commission, Little Rock; *Missouri Republican*, August 14, 1886.
5. (Marshall) *Texas Republican*, September 28, 1861; US War Department, *The War of the Rebellion*, 3: 745–746.
6. Nicholas Bartlett Pearce, "Arkansas Troops in the Battle of Wilson's Creek," *Battles and Leaders of the Civil War*, edited by Robert U. Johnson and C.C. Buel, 4 vols. (New York: Century, 1887), I: 299.
7. *Missouri Republican*, August 15, 1885.
8. *National Tribune*, October 28, 1886.
9. *Keokuk* (Iowa) *Daily Gate City*, August 14, 1884.
10. Ware, *The Lyon Campaign in Missouri*, 311.
11. *Muscatine Weekly*, August 30, 1861.
12. Watson, *Life in the Confederate Army*, 212.
13. Bell, "Price's Missouri Campaign, 1861," 318.
14. Robert H. Dacus, *Reminiscences of Company "H," First Arkansas Mounted Rifles* (Dardanelle, AR: Privately printed, 1897), n.p.

Chapter 12

1. *Keokuk Daily Gate City*, August 14, 1884.
2. Albert R. Greene, "On the Battle of Wilson's Creek," *Transactions of the Kansas State Historical Society, 1889–1896*, edited by F. G. Adams (Topeka: Press of the Kansas State Printing Co., 1896), 5: 116, 118–119. The original lyrics by Isaac Watts are "Am I a soldier of the cross / A follower of the Lamb/And shall I fear to own His cause / Or blush to speak His Name?" The parody refers instead to the notorious US Sen. James H. Lane of Kansas: "Am I a soldier of the boss / A follower of Jim Lane / And shall I fear to steal a horse / Or blush to ride the same?"
3. Richard W. Hatcher III and William Garrett Piston, *Kansans at Wilson's Creek: Soldiers' Letters from the Campaign for Southwest Missouri* (Springfield, MO: Wilson's Creek National Battlefield Foundation, 1993), 84. Along with editing this fine collection of newspaper correspondence, Piston and Hatcher produced the classic campaign study *Wilson's Creek: The Second Major Battle of the Civil War and the Men Who Fought It*, published by the University of North Carolina Press in 2000. This definitive account of the battle and its participants is required reading for any serious student of the Missouri Campaign of 1861. I owe an enormous debt of gratitude to both historians for their critical evaluation of this manuscript.
4. *National Tribune*, January 10, 1884.
5. Dailey, "In the Ranks under General Lyon," 587.
6. Ware, *The Lyon Campaign in Missouri*, 315–316.
7. John M. Schofield, *Forty-Six Years in the Army* (New York: Century Co., 1897), 42–43.
8. *National Tribune*, September 16, 1886.
9. Dailey, "In the Ranks under General Lyon in Missouri," 588.
10. It is entirely possible that Brigadier General McCulloch knew of Brigadier General Lyon's advance before his meeting with Major General Price. General Rains claimed to have sent a message to the army commander, while Lt. Buck Brown's patrol had returned to McCulloch's headquarters that morning and reported that they had blundered into advancing Federals. Although Colonel McIntosh believed that Brown's report was "another Missouri humbug," (a reference to Dug Springs), Brown emphatically replied, "No, not by a damned sight, Colonel." Before he returned to his camp, Lieutenant Brown had another heated encounter with the doubting McIntosh. Brown reported that McCulloch believed the report, however, as the general supposedly ordered an aide to warn Price and went in person to alert Capt. William Woodruff. If in fact McCulloch sent an aide to warn Price, he must have been delayed, because the Missouri commander reported only two messengers, both sent by Rains; if McCulloch himself warned

Woodruff, the latter did not mention that fact in his official report of the battle. A. V. Reiff, "History of 'Spy' Company, Raised at Fayetteville, Ark.," in *The War of the 'Sixties,* compiled by E. R. Hutchins (New York: Neale Publishing Co., 1912), 171–172.

11. *Missouri Republican,* August 21, 1861.
12. *Leavenworth* (Kansas) *Conservative,* August 29, 1861.
13. Hatcher and Piston, *Kansans at Wilson's Creek,* 84–87.
14. *National Tribune,* January 10, 1884.

Chapter 13

1. *Omaha* (Nebraska) *World-Herald,* September 15, 1901. R. J. Morris generously provided this little-used account of Lieutenant Ashby's role in the opening stages of the battle and Colonel Austin's death.
2. *Missouri Republican,* August 15, 1885.
3. *Arkansas True Democrat* (Little Rock), August 29, 1861. Dr. Cantrell related how a great many spoke of the execution of the battery and of the "scientific manner" in which its guns were handled.
4. W. E. Woodruff, *With the Light Guns in '61-'65: Reminiscences of Eleven Arkansas, Missouri, and Texas Light Batteries in the Civil War* (Little Rock: Central Printing Co., 1903), 38–45; *Missouri Republican,* August 15, 1885; *Arkansas True Democrat,* August 29, 1861.
5. Mudd, "What I Saw at Wilson's Creek," 95.
6. *Missouri Republican,* September 11, 1886.
7. *National Tribune,* November 10, 1892; August 22, 1901; August 6, 1903.
8. *Missouri Republican,* September 18, 1886.
9. Ibid., August 21, 1861.

Chapter 14

1. Capt. Clark Wright, commander of the two mounted Home Guard companies, operated with his unit independently of the regulars on the east side of Wilson's Creek and reported casualties of two men slightly wounded in the battle. Wright's report may be found in *The Missouri Republican* of August 22, 1861.
2. August 14, 1861, letter of J. A. Prudhomme, Company G, Third Louisiana, in undated newspaper clipping, Hulston Library, Wilson's Creek National Battlefield.
3. In his account of the fighting, Lt. Henry Clay Wood gave slightly different casualty figures (twenty killed and fifty-seven wounded, for a total of seventy-seven). US War Department, *The War of the Rebellion,* 1880–1901), 3: 72; *Missouri Republican,* August 21, 1861; Henry Clay Wood, "The Left of the Federal Line of Battle at Wilson's Creek," undated article in the files of Hulston Library, Wilson's Creek National Battlefield, 347.
4. The Zouave drill emphasized rapid movement, loading and firing in various positions, and "going to ground" while facing enemy fire, as opposed to the more formal parade-ground drill practiced by the majority of soldiers on both sides in 1861.

Chapter 15

1. *The Neosho* (Missouri) *Times,* August 15, 1901.
2. Reiff, "History of 'Spy' Company," 173.
3. Brigadier General Pearce's confusion is supported by his own account in *The Missouri Republican* of August 15, 1885, and in an account by Capt. J. G. McKean of the Fifth Arkansas, contained in the Hulston Library files. Pearce was not the only one confused by Colonel Sigel's men, however. An unidentified correspondent to the *Van Buren* (Arkansas) *Press* noted that Sigel's men appeared without colors and "wearing the badge of Missourians," so others were confused as to their true identity. *Daily Missouri Republican,* September 4, 1861.
4. Undated newspaper account of McKean, Fifth Arkansas, Hulston Library files.
5. *Missouri Republican,* August 15, 1885.
6. Other historians give a total of 297 casualties for Colonel Sigel's brigade (35 killed, 132 wounded, and 130 missing). A detailed study of the Compiled Service Records of the units in the brigade reveals the following statistics: Third Missouri—96 casualties (6 killed, 46 wounded, 2

mortally wounded, 4 missing, and 38 prisoners); Fifth Missouri—47 casualties (9 killed, 22 wounded, 1 mortally wounded, 7 missing, and 8 prisoners); and Backoff's Artillery—22 casualties (5 killed, 7 wounded, 6 missing, and 4 prisoners). Casualties in the US regular units are harder to determine. Capt. Eugene A. Carr, commander of Company I, First US Cavalry, claimed 4 men missing, while it appears that Company C, Second US Dragoons, lost 1 man missing in action. Another dragoon, possibly attached to Company C, was wounded.

Chapter 16

1. Wilkie, *The Iowa First*, 106
2. *National Tribune*, April 9, 1896.
3. *Muscatine Weekly Journal*, August 30, 1861.
4. Mudd, "What I Saw at Wilson's Creek," 97–100.
5. *Muscatine Weekly Journal*, August 30, 1861.
6. Wilkie, *The Iowa First*, 110.
7. *The Missouri Republican*, September 18, 1886.
8. *Muscatine Weekly Journal*, August 30, 1861.
9. *Atchison* (Kansas) *Freedom's Champion*, August 31, 1861.
10. US War Department, *The War of the Rebellion*, 3: 61.
11. *The Missouri Republican*, September 11, 1886.
12. Statement of Maj. Lucien J. Barnes, James Totten File, in "Letters Received by the Commission Branch of the Adjutant General's Office," National Archives.
13. John Dailey, "In the Ranks under General Lyon in Missouri—1861: The Observations of a Private Soldier," *Blue and Gray*, vol. 5 (1895), 199–202.
14. *Missouri Republican*, October 10, 1885.
15. W. O. Coleman, "Service of Col. W. O. Coleman," *Confederate Veteran*, vol. 19, no. 6 (June 1911), 285.
16. *Leavenworth Conservative*, August 29, 1861.
17. *National Tribune*, January 10, 1884.
18. Mudd, "What I Saw at Wilson's Creek," 98–100.
19. *Missouri Republican*, October 10, 1885. A State Guardsman remembered Weightman this way: "His judgment was good, he was kind to his men, and no braver man could be found." J. W. James, "Battle of Oak Hills, Mo.," *Confederate Veteran*, XXIV, no. 2 (February 1916), 72.
20. *Missouri Republican*, September 11, 1886.
21. *Muscatine Weekly Journal*, August 30, 1861.
22. Wilkie, *The Iowa First*, 114.
23. *Atchison Freedom's Champion*, August 24, August 31, 1861.
24. *National Tribune*, December 23, 1886.
25. Majors Schofield and Sturgis agreed, for the most part, with this popular view, although neither officer actually saw Brigadier General Lyon just before he died. Sturgis reported that he swung his hat in the air and called on the troops to follow him, whereas Schofield said he swung his hat in the air.
26. *National Tribune*, January 6, 1887; June 9, 1887; September 21, 1905. William Wherry, Brigadier General Lyon's aide, wrote his account of the general's death about the same time that Private Becher wrote his. Wherry remembered Lyon swinging his hat, but did not record any inspirational yell to the men. He also recalled Lyon slowly dismounting, falling into the arms of Lehmann, his orderly, and saying, "Lehmann, I am killed." We will probably never know the exact circumstances of Lyon's final minutes. William M. Wherry, "Wilson's Creek, and the Death of Lyon," *Battles and Leaders of the Civil War*, edited by Robert U. Johnson and C. C. Buel, 4 vols. (New York: Century, 1887), 1: 295.
27. *Daily Missouri Republican*, September 10, 1861.
28. US War Department, *The War of the Rebellion*, 3: 84.
29. *Dallas* (Texas) *Herald*, August 28, 1861.
30. *The Neosho* (Missouri) *Times*, August 15, 1901.
31. *National Tribune*, May 14, 1903.
32. *Daily Missouri Republican*, August 21, 1861.
33. US War Department, *The War of the Rebellion*, 3: 68.

Chapter 17

1. US War Department, *The War of the Rebellion*, 3: 62.
2. Wherry, "Wilson's Creek, and the Death of Lyon," I: 296–297.
3. Pearce, "Arkansas Troops in the Battle of Wilson's Creek," I: 302–303.
4. John R. Gratiot to editor, (Washington) *Arkansas Telegraph*, August 12, 1861, copy in Hulston Library files.
5. *Leavenworth Conservative*, August 29, 1861.
6. US War Department, *The War of the Rebellion*, 3: 62.
7. *Leavenworth Conservative*, August 29, 1861.
8. *National Tribune*, September 16, 1886.
9. *The Kansas State Journal* (Lawrence), August 29, 1861.
10. National Archives, M1098, *U.S. Army Generals' Reports of Civil War Service, 1864–1887*, vol. 9, Report 31, and *National Tribune*, August 29, 1895.
11. US War Department, *The War of the Rebellion*, 3: 85.
12. *National Tribune*, January 10, 1884.
13. US War Department, *The War of the Rebellion*, 3: 63.
14. *Muscatine Weekly Journal*, August 30, 1861.
15. *National Tribune*, January 10, 1884.
16. Mudd, "What I Saw at Wilson's Creek," 102.
17. *Missouri Republican*, October 10, 1885.
18. *National Tribune*, December 29, 1892.

Chapter 18

1. *Leavenworth Conservative*, August 29, 1861.
2. *National Tribune*, January 10, 1884.
3. Wilkie, *The Iowa First*, 114.
4. *Daily Missouri Republican*, August 18, 1861.
5. Although the traditional Federal casualty figure of 1,317 is used here, a recent compilation done by seasonal rangers at Wilson's Creek National Battlefield estimates the total number to be 1,096 casualties.
6. In an account for the *National Tribune*, Gen. Washington L. Elliott wrote that Major Sturgis relinquished command on August 10 because newspapers had reported Colonel Sigel's promotion to brigadier general of volunteers, thereby outranking every other Federal officer. As Sigel was commissioned only three days before the battle, it is unlikely that newspapers reached Springfield in time, but it is possible that a rumor was carried to town that he had in fact been promoted. *National Tribune*, August 16, 1883; *Weekly Missouri Democrat*, August 18, August 27, 1861.
7. (Springfield) *Missouri Weekly Patriot*, November 26, 1874.
8. *Missouri Republican*, August 18, August 20, 1861; *Weekly Missouri Democrat*, August 20, 1861.
9. (Marshall) *Texas Republican*, August 31, 1861.
10. Ibid., September 14, 1861.
11. The accepted Southern casualty figure is mentioned here, although recent work by seasonal rangers at Wilson's Creek National Battlefield estimates the losses to be far higher (1,386).
12. Mudd, "What I Saw at Wilson's Creek," 102–104.
13. *Arkansas True Democrat*, August 29, 1861.
14. Bell, "Price's Missouri Campaign, 1861," 416.
15. *National Tribune*, December 23, 1886.
16. *The Republican* (Lawrence, Kansas), August 29, 1861.
17. *Atchison Freedom's Champion*, August 24, 1861.
18. *National Tribune*, April 9, 1885.
19. J. W. James, "Battle of Oak Hills, Mo.," *Confederate Veteran*, vol. 24, no. 2 (February 1916), 72.
20. *Leavenworth Conservative*, August 29, 1861.
21. *The Kansas State Journal*, August 29, 1861.
22. *Atchison Freedom's Champion*, August 31, 1861.
23. *Atchison* (Kansas) *Daily Champion*, August 10, 1886.
24. US War Department, *The War of the Rebellion*, 3: 747.
25. Christopher Phillips, *Damned Yankee: The Life of General Nathaniel Lyon* (Columbia: University of Missouri Press, 1990), 263.

CREDITS

Cover   Andy Thomas (artist, www.andythomas.com) "Don't Yield an Inch," the Battle of Wilson's Creek.

Chapter 1   pg. 19, Claiborne Fox Jackson, Courtesy of *Battles and Leaders of the Civil War.*

Chapter 2   pg. 24, St. Louis "Turners," National Park Service, Wilson's Creek National Battlefield; pg. 26, Nathaniel Lyon, National Park Service, Wilson's Creek National Battlefield.

Chapter 4   pg. 41, William S. Harney, National Park Service, Wilson's Creek National Battlefield.

Chapter 5   pg. 55, John Marmaduke, National Park Service, Wilson's Creek National Battlefield; pg. 56, James Totten, National Park Service, Wilson's Creek National Battlefield; pg. 57, P. S. Alexander and S. W. Stone, National Park Service, Wilson's Creek National Battlefield.

Chapter 6   pg.62, Thomas Sweeny, National Park Service, Wilson's Creek National Battlefield; pg. 65, Greene County Courthouse, National Park Service, Wilson's Creek National Battlefield; pg. 74, John Taylor Hughes, National Park Service, Wilson's Creek National Battlefield.

Chapter 7   pg. 84, Arthur Gunther, National Park Service, Wilson's Creek National Battlefield.

Chapter 8   pg. 89, William Arnold, National Park Service, Wilson's Creek National Battlefield; pg. 91, Nicholas B. Pearce, National Park Service, Wilson's Creek National Battlefield.

Chapter 9   pg. 97, John C. Fremont, National Park Service, Wilson's Creek National Battlefield; pg. 103, James McIntosh, Courtesy of *Battles and Leaders of the Civil War*; pg. 109, Reuben Kay, National Park Service, Wilson's Creek National Battlefield; pg. 112, Wilson's Creek, National Park Service, Wilson's Creek National Battlefield.

Chapter 10   pg. 117, Joseph Plummer, Courtesy of National Archives.

Chapter 11   pg. 120, Wilson's Creek, distance, National Park Service, Wilson's Creek National Battlefield; pg. 123, Elkanah Greer, Courtesy of Miller's *Photographic History of the Civil War.*

Chapter 12   pg. 130, Frederick Steele, National Park Service, Wilson's Creek National Battlefield; pg. 133, Samuel Sturgis, National Park Service, Wilson's Creek National Battlefield; pg. 136, James McCown, National Park Service, Wilson's Creek National Battlefield.

Chapter 13   pg. 142-143, Wilson's Creek, panorama, Courtesy of *Battles and Leaders of the Civil War.*

Chapter 14   pg. 151, Ray House, National Park Service, Wilson's Creek National Battlefield.

Chapter 15   pg. 163, Dr. Samuel Melcher, Courtesy of Memorials of Deceased Companions, Illinois Commandery, Military Order of the Loyal Legion of the U.S.

Chapter 16   pg. 170, Jeremiah Cockrell, National Park Service, Wilson's Creek National Battlefield; pg. 177, John B. Clark, National Park Service, Wilson's Creek National Battlefield; pg. 180, Robert Byington Mitchell, National Park Service, Wilson's Creek National Battlefield.

Chapter 17   pg. 183, William Wherry, National Park Service, Wilson's Creek National Battlefield.

Chapter 18   pg. 190, Springfield, National Park Service, Wilson's Creek National Battlefield; pg. 196, Stone cairn, National Park Service, Wilson's Creek National Battlefield; pg. 197, Peter J. Osterhaus, National Park Service, Wilson's Creek National Battlefield.

Maps   Created by Donald S. Frazier.

INDEX